101
INVESTMENT
TIPS

Prentice
Hall
Canada

A Pearson Company

Toronto

Canadian Cataloguing in Publication Data

Vos, Willem, 1972-
101 investment tips: how to maximize returns and reduce risk

Includes index.
ISBN 0-13-031107-3

1. Investments. 2. Finance, Personal. I. Helik, James II. Title. III. Title: One hundred and one investment tips.

HG4521.V67 2000   332.6   C00-931467-9

ISBN 0-13-031107-3

Editorial Director, Trade Division: Andrea Crozier
Acquisitions Editor: Paul Woods
Copy Editor: Catharine Haggert
Production Editor: Lori McLellan
Art Direction: Mary Opper
Interior Design: Gary Beelik
Production Manager: Kathrine Pummell
Page Layout: Dave McKay

1 2 3 4 5 WC 04 03 02 01 00

Printed and bound in Canada.

This publication contains the opinions and ideas of its authors and is designed to provide useful advice in regard to the subject matter covered. The authors and publisher are not engaged in rendering legal, accounting, or other professional services in this publication. This publication is not intended to provide a basis for action in particular circumstances without consideration by a competent professional. The authors, their employees and the publisher expressly disclaim any responsibility for any liability, loss, or risk, personal or otherwise, which is incurred as a consequence, directly or indirectly, of the use and application of any of the contents of this book.

Visit the Prentice Hall Canada Web site! Send us your comments, browse our catalogues, and more. **www.phcanada.com**.

A Pearson Company

Dedication

To Jenny Lynn:
Thank you.
W.V.
To Owen Thomas and Meredith Margaret:
Thanks for putting up with Dad
J.H.

Contents

Acknowledgments

First I would like to thank Jim for his hard work and contribution to this book. Without your help I would never have completed this project. Your countless hours and enthusiasm do not go unnoticed or unappreciated. Thank you Jim!

I would like to thank my colleagues at TALFund for their encouragement, especially Jean Lefebvre who never fails to enlighten me with his words of wisdom.

Thanks for all the people at Prentice Hall: Paul Woods, Andrea Crozier, Michael Bubna, Jennifer Matyczak, Lori McLellan, Catherine Dorton and Martin Litkowski, just to name a few.

To my family and friends, thank you for you patience and understanding. And I thank God for giving me the ability and skill to complete this project.

W.V.

Thanks go to Wilfred, for all of his ideas and for the original concept of the book.

Thanks as well to Ana Bassios, for the freedom to study everything from real estate dynamics to the future of the financial services industry, and to Ron Cluett and Stephen Bearne—two people who are far too practical to be called academics.

To the many people who, often unknowingly, provided encouragement along the way—Kathryn Baus, Dale Ennis, Victor Estevan, John McLaine and David Rudd— my appreciation.

Thanks to Cat Haggert for turning a bunch of pages into a book.

Finally, it is typical in these matters to thank your spouse, but in this case it is really merited. This book was written around the birth of our second child. When I asked my wife, "Hey, why don't I take some time off work…and write a book," she only paused briefly before saying yes. So I'm done now, it's time to change the diapers.

J.H.

Introduction

Will you achieve the financial security you want? Planning for your financial future can make the difference between just getting by and peace of mind. However, it is often hard enough to plan the family vacation, let alone plan for some financial dream that is twenty or more years away. Thus, many people close their eyes, make a Registered Retirement Savings Plan (RRSP) contribution, add a little bit of financial planning, and hope for the best. This is an excellent start, but tweaking things just a little will allow you to make significant improvements to what you have already begun. This book will give you ideas and tips on starting your financial plan as well as maintaining and tuning it through your financial lifetime. Read on! There is some great information in this book—you won't be disappointed.

To get started, we first deal with calculating what you are worth and creating a budget to aid your investing. We also set out the reasons behind starting this whole process as early as you can, and help you establish realistic expectations, build a better portfolio, and find a good financial planner.

The tips in this book will also help you fit your home into your financial plan, examine whether it is a good investment, how to find a better mortgage, and how to get income from your home at retirement. We also cover your RRSP, how to profit from it, how to make better use of it, and how it fits within your financial plan. We also discuss important tips around retirement and how to handle the transition from work to retirement.

A good proportion of this book covers the growing and changeable mutual fund industry. With more mutual funds available than there are stocks listed on the Toronto Stock Exchange, this book tells you how to separate the good from the bad and how to make the choice that is right for you. Most importantly, it notes that there are now funds available for even the most specialized and aggressive investor. We cover everything from conservative income mutual funds to specialty funds that invest in everything from emerging countries to the Internet.

But there is more to the investment world than just mutual funds. We offer tips about bonds, the new index units, stocks and the many approaches to buying them, futures, and options to name just a few. After discussing various investment options we advise how to find the best discount broker, how to place better buy and sell orders, how to profit from market anomalies and investment strategies such as momentum investing, and how to profit from market declines. Then we focus on the tax treatment of investments and how taxes will influence some of your investment decisions. While all of these investments can make you money, we also outline ways to save some money by maximizing your investment dollar.

We hope you find our tips valuable, and we look forward to receiving your comments at www.bestofbaystreet.com.

Wilfred Vos & Jim Helik

1

One

Getting Started

How do you feel? You hear this questions frequently when you are sick, but it is also a question you should ask yourself about your investments. It is one of the most important questions, yet it is rarely asked. How you feel when capital markets jump up and down will affect how you make investment decisions. How you feel about spending your money will determine how much you can afford to invest, and how you feel about choosing only a limited amount of investments or diversifying your money across a broader spectrum of investment options will all have an impact on your long-term financial freedom.

This chapter will examine how you can get started in the financial world—an area that some people find overly complex. First we get you in the starting block by calculating your net worth, which doesn't have to be an exact number-crunching exercise. A rough, back-of-the-envelope calculation is sufficient for you to understand where you currently stand. Then we will quickly move into creating a budget to determine how you are spending your money and how much you can afford to invest. We will motivate you to start investing early, find yourself a personal financial planner, build a better portfolio, and set realistic expectations for your investment portfolio.

Before we get started, we want to provide a quick note on insurance, which is the first thing that some people think of when they speak of financial planning. First, don't buy life insurance if you don't need it. By and large, the purpose of life insurance is to protect dependents in case of premature death. If this doesn't fit your profile, which basically means if you are young and childless, or if you are older with grown children, you don't need life insurance. Second, don't buy more insurance than you need, but buy enough to let you sleep at night. While many calculations can be performed to determine an insurance amount, think in terms of what will be needed to provide for your dependents over and above your existing assets, rather than picking an arbitrary multiple of your salary, or a nice round figure like half a million dollars.

The cost of your insurance will depend on a number of factors, including your gender, age, general health, whether or not you smoke, and any particular factors that are requirements of the policy (such as inflation protection or the period of a fixed term). Annual premiums do vary, so it pays to compare—this is where you can save big dollars. One source for term life comparisons is found at http://www.term4sale.com or http://www.termforsale.com, which can provide cost comparisons based on the factors you enter into the web site. Most people should stick to the basics of term insurance especially if you are young—term insurance is the cheapest insurance available.

Applying this principle and the following investment tips will be a useful process that will certainty pay dividends both today and tomorrow. So let's get started.

What Are You Worth?

Tip 1

SUPPOSE YOU WANT TO TAKE YOUR FAMILY TO FLORIDA, OR YOUR SPOUSE ON

A ROMANTIC CRUISE TO THE CARIBBEAN, AND YOU CALL YOUR TRAVEL AGENT

TO MAKE SOME ARRANGEMENTS. THE TRAVEL AGENT IS GOING TO ASK YOU

SEVERAL QUESTIONS:

- When would you like to go on your vacation?
- Where would you like to go?
- How much would you like to spend?
- What type of accommodation are you looking for?

An investor should ask similar questions. It is important to understand where you are today from a financial perspective. It is also important to know where you want to be in the future, and the financial resources you currently have to reach your objectives. Where you are today is measured by your net worth, where you want to be is defined by your goals and objectives. Your financial plan will provide the road map and get you from where you are to where you want to be.

Your financial goals and objectives can range from travelling to educating your children. Once you have established your goals you can determine where you are today in relation to these goals. Your net worth, which is equal to your assets (all the things you own, including a house or car) minus all the money you still owe (mortgage, credit cards, student loans), tells you your current standing (where you are today). Let's get started by calculating your net worth—once you have calculated this you can determine an appropriate strategy for achieving your financial goals.

Your net worth:

- provides a starting point

- allows you to prepare a strategy to achieve your goals and objectives

- allows you to measure your progress every time you update your net worth

- provides a guideline and instills financial discipline

- gives you an idea of the resources you have at your disposal.

The process of calculating your net worth begins with collecting all the relevant data. You should have a good idea of what your house and car are worth, and the amounts that you owe on credit cards, personal loans, and on your mortgage. Gathering all this data isn't fun, but the result is a financial snapshot that you can use for other facets of financial planning such as tax, estate, and retirement planning. Here is one simple example, which can be adapted for your own circumstances.

THE NET WORTH STATEMENT OF JACK AND JILL HILL AS OF DECEMBER 31, 2000

ASSETS			LIABILITIES		
Liquid Assets	Short Term				
Cash	$ 5 000	1.8%	Credit Card	$ 1 250	0.4%
Money Market Fund	$ 15 000	5.3%	Line of Credit	$ 2 500	0.9%
Investment Assets	Long Term				
RRSPs	$ 45 000	15.8%	Mortgage	$145 000	50.9%
Shares of Bell Canada	$ 35 000	12.3%	Total Liabilities	$148 750	52.2%
Personal Assets					
House	$185 000	64.9%	Net Worth	$136 250	47.8%
Total Assets	$285 000	100%	Total Liabilities and Net Worth	$285 000	100%

Your Budget

Tip 2

DID YOU EVER WRITE A CHEQUE OR USE YOUR CREDIT CARD AND THEN HOPE THAT THE CHEQUE WOULDN'T BOUNCE OR THE CREDIT CARD WOULDN'T GET DENIED? SOME MODEST PLANNING WILL ENSURE THAT YOU DON'T HAVE TO WORRY ABOUT YOUR CREDIT OR PAY UNNECESSARY CHEQUE CHARGES OR INTEREST ON YOUR CREDIT CARD.

A budget or a cash flow statement will help you to determine the "flow" of your money from one period of time to another. You will need to determine what money you are getting, and what you are spending. It is more important to go through the process than to track every last penny, so if you don't know the details about a particular item give it your best guess. Based on the information in your cash flow statement you can determine your rates of spending and saving and whether your savings are enough for you to meet your long-term financial goals. On the outflow side, this statement can also be used to review your spending habits. If you spend more than you earn you can use your budget to review your discretionary spending and see how your current situation can be reversed.

Many investors find it useful to prepare a monthly budget, as many expenses are paid on a monthly basis. In the example below we see that Jack and Jill Hill have the ability to save $550 per month, which should increase their net worth over time.

MONTHLY CASH FLOW ESTIMATES FOR JACK AND JILL HILL

	JANUARY	FEBRUARY	...	DECEMBER	TOTAL
Income					
Employment, Dividends, Interest	$ 3 500	$ 3 500	...	$ 3 500	$ 42 000
Expenses					
Food, Clothing, etc.	$ 650	$ 650	...	$ 650	$ 7 800
Mortgage, Tax, etc.	$ 1 700	$ 1 700	...	$ 1 700	$ 20 400
Debts, Insurance	$ 350	$ 350	...	$ 350	$ 4 200
Vacation, Entertainment, etc.	$ 250	$ 250	...	$ 250	$ 3 000
Income Minus Expenses	$ 550	$ 550	...	$ 550	$ 6 600

By examining your budget over time you may determine that your net worth is not growing rapidly enough. You then have some choices: you can curtail your spending, increase your income, or a combination of both in order to increase net worth. To improve your current cash flow situation consider:

- Restrain your spending on "small" items. A daily cup of coffee or lunches out add up. Consider tracking what you spend on such items in a sample month to determine if this is how you want to spend your money.

- Economize on purchases. Avoid convenience shopping and buy in bulk whenever feasible.

- Negotiate prices on everything.

- Restructure your debt. Pay off your most expensive debt first, which is typically credit card debt.

How to Profit from Your Record Keeping

Tip 3

INFORMATION IS ONE OF THE KEYS TO PROFIT. NATURALLY YOU HAVE TO KNOW WHAT MONEY IS COMING IN. BUT IF YOU TRACK WHERE YOUR MONEY IS GOING, YOU CAN MORE EASILY ADJUST OR REDUCE YOUR MONTHLY EXPENDITURES WITHOUT CHANGING YOUR LIFESTYLE. ALL YOU NEED ARE FIVE STATEMENTS TO DETERMINE HOW YOU ARE MAKING AND SPENDING YOUR MONEY. YOU NEED YOUR CREDIT CARD BILL, A MONTHLY BANK STATEMENT, YOUR T4 STATEMENT, YOUR CANADA CUSTOMS AND REVENUE AGENCY NOTICE OF ASSESSMENT (WHICH YOU RECEIVE AFTER YOU FILE YOUR INCOME TAX), AND YOUR INVESTMENT STATEMENT FROM YOUR BROKER OR MUTUAL FUND COMPANY.

Your credit card can become one of your most valuable tools in your personal financial plan. The credit card provides you with free credit on a short-term basis, if you pay the balance in full every month. The many cards in the marketplace make it appealing to make as many of your purchases as possible on plastic, to collect the various air miles, cash rebates, or other points that are available. Just as importantly, the monthly statement will provide you with most of the information you need to track your monthly spending.

The next important piece of paper is your bank statement. It will fill in the holes that the credit card statement doesn't answer. You can examine your bank statement to see how often you used an ATM or how much you spent with direct and preauthorized payments. It is a good idea to establish as many pre-authorized payments as possible including the gas bill, the hydro bill, and your mortgage. You should try to pay for all your bills using your credit card, pre-authorized payments, and debit card transactions and then easily track all your expenses with the exception of some spending money.

Your T4, which is provided by your employer, will provide you with your taxable income in a year and all the applicable deductions made on your behalf by your employer. After you complete your taxes you will receive a Canada Customs and Revenue Agency Notice of Assessment, which will provide a summary of your taxes, credits, and RRSP contribution room.

Your last vital statement comes from your investment broker or mutual fund company. This statement will provide you with essential information such as how much money you have made from your investments, what and where you have invested, what your average purchase cost is, and whether you have unrealized gains or losses.

Keep all these statements in one place where you can access them easily. At the end of each month you will be able to determine how much money came in and how much money went out of your bank account, and more importantly, where it all went. It is worth your while to spend some time with these statements to understand your earning, spending, and investing to make adjustments that can benefit you in the short and long term.

Setting Your Goals

Tip 4

THE KEY TO SUCCESSFUL FINANCIAL PLANNING IS KNOWING WHERE YOU WANT
TO GO—YOU CAN DESCRIBE YOUR FINANCIAL DESTINATION. ONCE YOU KNOW
THAT, YOU CAN FIGURE OUT THE STRATEGIES TO GET YOU THERE. THE FOLLOW-
ING STEPS WILL HELP TO DEFINE YOUR GOALS.

STEP 1: LIST YOUR GOALS—AND WHEN YOU WANT TO ACHIEVE THEM

In this first step, focus on writing down the actual goal, not the means of achieving the goal.
For example, "I want to have a million dollars" is actually the method of achieving a goal
such as retiring early, or paying off the mortgage. To make your life easier, stick to those
goals that are clear, realistic, and achievable. Different people will have different goals as
well as priorities for these goals. Each person's list will depend on many unique factors. Your
list could read like the following:

- retiring when I'm 55

- paying off my debts before I'm 55

- buying a house before I'm 30

- travelling with my spouse before I'm 50

- running my own business before I'm 45.

STEP 2: WHAT DOES IT COST?

Your next step is to determine the costs associated with each of your goals. In some cases this might be a relatively modest monthly figure (buying a car, for example). In other cases this might be a larger, but still easily definable lump sum (i.e., paying off the mortgage). In still other cases, the amount of money involved is a little more nebulous (i.e., retiring early), which might result in your redefining or clarifying your goal (i.e. retire by age 55). Match the funds you will need to the time in your life you will need them to achieve your goal(s), and don't forget to add the costs of your goals together.

STEP 3: WHAT DO YOU HAVE?

Go back to your net worth statement and determine what you have now—how far along are you to the goal of paying down your mortgage? If you do not have enough money today, you will have to implement a saving/investing plan to achieve this goal or adapt your financial goals.

STEP 4: GET ON THE PLAN

You now know where you are and where you want to go. Examine and implement the tips and strategies throughout this book to allow you to realize your financial goals.

STEP 5: MONITOR YOUR PROGRESS

Your progress to your goals should be checked along the way. You want to ensure that your actions are matching your priorities. Similarly, you want to periodically check on your results as well as your actions—dutifully saving money monthly may not be enough if your investment actions don't result in the funds you need to finance your goals.

Managing your financial plans is a continuous process of goal setting, monitoring, and making the changes necessary along the way. Every once in a while revisit your goals and feel free to adapt either them or your strategy.

Goal Setting—Pulling Your
Net Worth and Your Budget Together

Tip 5

MANY PEOPLE PAY THEIR BILLS AT THE END OF THE MONTH AND INVEST WHAT-
EVER IS LEFT OVER, IF ANYTHING. HOWEVER, INVESTORS SHOULD REALIZE THAT
SAVINGS INCREASE YOUR NET WORTH BY EITHER INCREASING YOUR ASSETS
THROUGH INVESTMENT OR REDUCING YOUR DEBTS THROUGH EARLY REPAY-
MENT, OR A COMBINATION OF BOTH. YOU HAVE TO TREAT SAVINGS AS A FIXED
EXPENSE, AND "PAY YOURSELF FIRST" TO ACHIEVE YOUR OWN FINANCIAL
OBJECTIVES. THIS MEANS MAKING INVESTMENT SAVINGS A PART OF YOUR
BUDGET, RATHER THAN SOMETHING THAT IS DONE WITH MONEY THAT IS LEFT
OVER.

From the previous tips in this chapter you have determined your net worth and where you
spend your money. Let's tie your net worth and budget together to map out how to achieve
your financial goal. You should be able to define your investment goal and determine how
much saving is necessary in order to achieve that goal. For example, if investor Jill Hill
wants to retire at 65 with $1 million, she has $100 000 today and estimates that she can

earn 10 per cent per year, and she is currently 50, she will have to save an additional $18 326 per year to meet her goal. If Jill is saving less than this amount, she will either have to alter her spending in order to achieve this objective, or else change the goal.

The next step is saving the money in order to achieve your goal. In the above example Jill has to save $18 326 per year and her budget will help her determine where the money will come from.

When you are doing this exercise yourself, there are several strategies that you can utilize in order to increase your savings rate.

- Take 10 per cent of your income and invest it off the top, then adjust all your other expenditures accordingly. This could be considered a large step initially, but if implemented successfully you should be assured a more comfortable lifestyle if you start at an early age. One way to do this is with an automatic savings plan. Automatic savings plans deduct money from your paycheque or withdraw money from your bank account and invest the amount before you ever see it. To find out more about automatic investment plans ask your employer or visit your bank branch.

- On the other hand, you could start small—contributing $50, $100, or $150 per month to your savings. If you start with an aggressive goal and you have a hard time meeting your current financial obligations you are far more likely to get frustrated. Once you have established a routine, then increase your savings rate periodically.

- Think about saving rather than spending. Of course this is easier said than done, but try to integrate the idea of saving today and spending tomorrow (rather than the other way around) into your lifestyle.

- Indulge periodically. If you achieve a goal then reward yourself.

Don't Forget About Inflation

Tip 6

THE BASIC CONCEPT BEHIND SAVINGS IS DELAYED GRATIFICATION—IF YOU INVEST AND DEFER PURCHASING GOODS AND SERVICES TODAY YOU SHOULD BE ABLE TO PURCHASE MORE GOODS AND SERVICES IN THE FUTURE, EVEN IF THE PRICE OF THESE GOODS INCREASES IN VALUE. HOWEVER, SAVING FOR ITS OWN SAKE ISN'T NECESSARILY GOOD. IT IS IMPORTANT TO EARN HIGHER RATES OF RETURN (OFTEN HIGHER THAN GOOD OLD, SAFE GICS), OTHERWISE YOU WOULD BE BETTER OFF SPENDING ALL OF YOUR MONEY TODAY.

Inflation is the reason we should pursue more aggressive returns. Inflation refers to the price increase of a general basket of goods and services. It is generally measured by the Consumer Price Index (CPI). The CPI tracks the price of everything from a gallon of gasoline to food. We have to consider the level of inflation because inflation erodes our purchasing power by making the cost of goods higher.

As an example, assume that you have $1000 and you go to the store to purchase a stereo, which costs $1000. Upon entering the store you decided you wanted to invest the money for one year instead. You invest your money at 5 per cent, and at the end of the year you have $1050. You then return to the store in order to buy the stereo for $1000. While this seemed like a great idea—you would forgo the purchase for one year in order to increase your purchasing power by $50—you return to the store only to find out that the selling price for the stereo has increased to $1100. Disappointed, you pull an extra $50 out of your wallet and buy the stereo.

The price of the stereo has increased dramatically because inflation at the time was 10 per cent. Currently, inflation is not at 10 per cent, but during the 1980s there were periods when inflation was at least at that level. High inflation will encourage consumers to spend today instead of saving.

Investors should always make sure that they have the ability to earn a rate of return greater than inflation. The rate of return that you earn, minus the rate of inflation, is approximately equal to your real rate of return. The real rate of return is the rate at which your purchasing power actually increases. If you invested $1000 for one year and earned a real rate of return of 5 per cent you would have the ability to purchase an additional $50 worth of goods and services. In addition, investors should realize that they have to pay taxes on their investment gains, which will also reduce the real rate of return.

Earning a return greater than inflation will ensure that you increase your purchasing power, and have the ability to consume more products and services that you couldn't otherwise afford before you began to invest.

Start Early: It Makes a Big Difference

Tip 7

IN BUSINESS THERE IS AN OLD SAYING: "IF YOU FAIL TO PLAN YOU ARE PLAN-NING TO FAIL." AT WORK, ASTUTE BUSINESSPEOPLE SPEND A GREAT DEAL OF TIME PLANNING AND THEN IMPLEMENTING THEIR COMPANY'S BUSINESS STRAT-EGY. THE STRENGTHS AND WEAKNESS OF THEIR ORGANIZATION ARE EXAMINED AND THE OPPORTUNITIES AND THREATS OF THEIR INDUSTRY ARE ASSESSED. THEN, AN APPROPRIATE BUSINESS STRATEGY IS IDENTIFIED, ARTICULATED, AND IMPLEMENTED. HOWEVER, MANY INDIVIDUALS FAIL TO IMPLEMENT SUCH A PRUDENT STRATEGY FOR THEIR PERSONAL FINANCES. YOU DON'T HAVE TO CREATE A DETAILED BUSINESS PLAN FOR YOUR PERSONAL FINANCES TO MEET YOUR GOALS AND OBJECTIVES, BUT YOU DO NEED TO IMPLEMENT SOME KIND OF PLAN. THE BEST PLAN YOU COULD FOLLOW IS TO START INVESTING EARLY. BUT DON'T GET DISCOURAGED IF YOU HAVEN'T STARTED YET. THE BEST TIME TO HAVE PLANTED A TREE WAS 20 YEARS AGO, BUT THE NEXT BEST TIME IS TODAY.

The early starters usually outpace those who come to the gate late. The differences are dramatic. For example, Jack and Jill Hill have both contributed or are planning to contribute to an RRSP for retirement. However, Jill was an early starter, who opened an RRSP at age 20 and put $2000 per year into her RRSP until age 30 for a total of $20 000. Jill never made another contribution but let her investment grow until age 55. Jack is a late starter, who didn't open an RRSP until age 30, just when Jill stopped her annual RRSP contributions. Each and every year, without missing one contribution, Jack continued to contribute $2000 to his RRSP until the age of 55, for a total of $52 000 invested. If both Jack and Jill were to earn 10 per cent on their investments throughout their life until age 55, Jill would have accumulated almost $402 000, and Jack would have accumulated over $218 000. Jack would have had less money than Jill, and he would have contributed $32 000 more money into his RRSP. Jack never caught up with Jill, while Jill realized that a compounded tax-deferred investment is one of the most powerful ways to accumulate money for your retirement.

Consider the following table. An investor who invested $50 per month for 25 years will have a total of $66 342 after 5 years. An investor who invested $300 per month for 25 years will have an investment portfolio of $398 050 after 25 years. Squeezing out a little more to invest every month, and letting that growth compound, makes a real difference.

GROWTH OF REGULAR SAVINGS PLAN AT 10 PER CENT PER YEAR.

MONTHLY INVESTMENT	NUMBER OF YEARS				
	5	10	15	20	25
$50	$ 3 872	$ 10 242	$ 20 724	$ 37 968	$ 66 342
$100	$ 7 744	$ 20 484	$ 41 447	$ 75 937	$ 132 683
$150	$ 11 616	$ 30 727	$ 62 171	$ 113 905	$ 199 025
$200	$ 15 487	$ 40 969	$ 82 894	$ 151 874	$ 265 367
$250	$ 19 359	$ 51 211	$ 103 618	$ 189 842	$ 331 708
$300	$ 23 231	$ 61 453	$ 124 341	$ 227 811	$ 398 050

Starting early will also allow you to increase your risk tolerance, because over the long term a risky investment's short-term gains will offset its short-term losses. Thus, long-term investors are not as reluctant to invest in more risky investments. Investors who are able to increase their time-horizon will benefit from higher rates of return.

How to Select
the Right Financial Planner for You

Tip 8

DURING THE PAST DECADE THE FINANCIAL PLANNING INDUSTRY EARNED A REPU-

TATION AS BEING A PRODUCT-BASED INDUSTRY, WITH INVESTMENT VEHICLES AS

THE PRODUCTS. INDIVIDUALS CALLING THEMSELVES FINANCIAL PLANNERS SPENT

LITTLE TIME PLANNING AND A LOT OF TIME "PUSHING A PRODUCT" TO

INVESTORS. FINANCIAL PLANNERS WERE NOT SOLELY TO BLAME. THE MUTUAL

FUND INDUSTRY WAS GROWING AT AN ANNUAL RATE OF 30 PER CENT PER YEAR,

AND INVESTORS WERE DEMANDING PRODUCT AND PRODUCT INFORMATION.

Recently the financial planning industry has made several dramatic changes. The industry has transformed itself into a profession that provides total wealth management, including comprehensive planning and advice service. A comprehensive financial plan is actually more important than the investments that you make. Therefore you should find a good planner who can develop a comprehensive financial plan and ensure that you have a good plan to meet your financial objectives.

A good financial planner can make or save you hundreds or thousands of dollars a year. However, most investors find it difficult to find a good financial planner, and sometimes they only find out that the financial planner they are dealing with isn't right for them after it is too late. So, what should investors be looking for in a good financial planner? First of all, make sure that they are financial planners in the first place. Have they been in the industry for more than a couple of months? Most importantly, do they have the qualifications to do the job right? Anyone can call himself or herself a financial planner, so make sure they have an actual designation behind them. The standard is a CFP (Certified Financial Planner), but there is also the RFP (Register Financial Planner), which the Canadian Association of Financial Planners grants, the CFC (Chartered Financial Consultant), and the CIM (Canadian Investment Management). These are just a few, and there are also other designations that relate to investment management or insurance.

Don't hire the first person you talk to; you may choose them in the end but don't pick them before talking with at least a couple of other individuals. This is the most important thing that you can do. To get a list of potential candidates you can ask for referrals from friends and relatives, or you can also talk to a mutual fund company, your local bank or credit union, insurance agent, attorney, or tax preparer.

You can also ask your financial planner for client referrals, and you want to see if there is a good personal fit with your own character.

Make sure the planner you work with has knowledge of investments, estate planning, and tax planning. Don't expect a fortune-teller who can propel you into instant riches. Instead, expect a competent individual who can help you achieve your financial goals by developing a comprehensive financial plan.

How to Build a Better Portfolio

Tip 9

ASSET ALLOCATION IS A FANCY TERM THAT REFERS TO THE DISTRIBUTION OF YOUR INVESTMENT FUNDS TO BROAD CATEGORIES OF INVESTMENT CATEGORIES. IT TRACKS HOW MUCH YOU INVEST, AND WHERE. ASSET ALLOCATION IS BY FAR THE MOST IMPORTANT DETERMINANT OF PORTFOLIO PERFORMANCE. A 1986 STUDY CONDUCTED BY BRINSON, HOOD, AND BEEBOWER FOUND THAT 95 PER CENT OF THE VARIANCE OF AN INVESTMENT PORTFOLIO WAS THE RESULT OF THE ASSET ALLOCATION DECISIONS. THUS, ONE OF THE BIGGEST CONTRIBUTORS TO PORTFOLIO PERFORMANCE IS NOT WHICH FUNDS YOU INVEST IN OVER THE LONG-TERM, BUT WHAT YOUR INVESTMENT MIX IS. SAID DIFFERENTLY, IT IS MORE IMPORTANT TO INVEST THE RIGHT AMOUNT OF YOUR PORTFOLIO IN U.S. EQUITIES, FOR EXAMPLE, THAN TO INVEST IN THE BEST U.S. MUTUAL FUND OVER THE LONG-TERM BUT TO ONLY ALLOCATE A SMALL PORTION OF YOUR PORTFOLIO TO THAT TOP FUND.

The largest reason why investors differ in their portfolio makeup is due to a difference in risk tolerance. Once you have determined your risk you can more easily determine what your asset mix should be. One straightforward system for the evaluation of the risk and reward trade-off is found in the questionnaire below. Investors with a high score (above 30) are more aggressive and could build a more equity-oriented investment portfolio. Investors with a low score should consider less risky investments for their investment portfolio.

INVESTMENT OBJECTIVE

Strongly Agree (5); Agree (4); Neutral (3); Disagree (2); Strongly Disagree (1);

1. Earning a high long-term rate of return that will allow my investment to grow faster than inflation is a very important objective for me. 5 4 3 2 1

2. I would like an investment that provides me with an opportunity to defer taxation of capital gains and/or interest income to future years. 5 4 3 2 1

3. I do not require a high level of current income from my investments. 5 4 3 2 1

4. My major investment goals are relatively long-term. 5 4 3 2 1

5. I am willing to tolerate sharp up and down swings in the return on my investment in order to seek a potentially higher return than would normally be expected from more stable investments. 5 4 3 2 1

6. I am willing to risk a short-term loss in return for a potentially higher long-run rate of return. 5 4 3 2 1

7. I am financially able to accept a low level of liquidity in my investment portfolio. 5 4 3 2 1

Source: William G. Droms, Copyright © 1988.

Once you have completed the questionnaire simply add your answers for all the questions. Then check your score on the table below. Getting the asset mix right is important because it will ensure you make the most money.

SCORE	ASSET CLASS								
	Cash	Bonds	High Yield Bonds	Balanced	Domestic Equity	Global Equity	U.S. Equity	International Equity	Historical Return
5	95%	5%							8.56%
15	40%	25%	1%	18%	4%	12%			10.37%
25		25%	12%	6%	21%		16%	20%	11.89%
30		15%	10%		27%		22%	26%	12.27%
35		5%	5%		32%		27%	31%	12.59%

When You Own Too Many Investments

Tip 10

REMEMBER WHEN YOU WERE A KID AND YOU STARTED COLLECTING BARBIE DOLLS OR HOCKEY CARDS? EACH YEAR YOU GOT MORE AND MORE AND A FEW YEARS LATER YOU HAD A REAL COLLECTION. THE SAME THING HAS HAPPENED TO INVESTORS WHO BEGAN INVESTING IN MUTUAL FUNDS DURING THE PAST DECADE, AND WHO HAVE SEEN THEIR COLLECTION GROW TO THE POINT WHERE THEY NOW HAVE 10 TO 15 FUNDS. BUT WHILE THERE MAY BE REAL VALUE IN A COLLECTION OF HOCKEY CARDS, HAVING TOO MANY MUTUAL FUNDS MAY NOT ADD VALUE TO YOUR PORTFOLIO.

Understanding how many investments are needed in a portfolio has been an intrinsic element in the investing process since the 1950s when economist Harry Markowitz showed mathematically exactly how diversification reduced volatility without sacrificing return by investing in investments that go up and down at different times. This process of constructing a portfolio with the highest return for a given level of risk was called "mean variance optimization" and has come to be known as Modern Portfolio Theory (MPT).

It is important to diversify your portfolio to spread risk, but it is also important to ensure that your portfolio has some "fuel" to propel your investments upwards.

Here are some tips to determine if you have invested in too many mutual funds:

- Every time you invest in a mutual fund you invest $1000 or less.

- When you receive your client statement it is more than three pages long.

- Most of your investments move together depending on the broad economy or market forces.

- You have never sold a mutual fund in your life.

It is a delicate balance to find the right number of mutual funds, but finding that balance can be very profitable. In addition to MPT, another approach is found in Relative Portfolio Theory (RPT). The objective behind RPT is to deliver consistent predictable performance after 12 months relative to other investments. It aims to add value by creating a combination of investments that outperform the average mutual fund consistently after 12 months. RPT creates an optimal portfolio of funds that perform well because the investments do not rise or fall in value together.

RPT optimizes a portfolio of funds over various time frames and ensures that in the short term and long term the investor incurs the least amount of risk. Conversely, MPT creates an optimal portfolio of funds over the long term, but investors still incur short-term risk. For some up-to-date RPT data on funds, check out *The Best of the Best* by Wilfred Vos and Bruce McDougall.

Have Realistic Expectations

Tip 11

THE PUBLISHED LISTS OF THE RICH AND FAMOUS CAN SOMETIMES MAKE INSTRUCTIVE READING. OF THE 500 RICHEST PEOPLE IN THE UNITED STATES ONLY WARREN BUFFETT, THE LEGENDARY VALUE INVESTOR, BUILT HIS NET WORTH BY INVESTING IN OTHER COMPANIES. THE OTHER INDIVIDUALS BUILT THEIR NET WORTH BY HOLDING THE BULK OF THEIR INVESTMENTS IN ONE COMPANY—THE COMPANY THEY OWNED. THEY HAVE THE CONVICTION TO FOCUS THEIR ENERGIES AND RESOURCES IN ONE AREA.

In other words, to have a superior longer-term performance (the kind of performance you need to become a billionaire), you must be able to undertake the risks associated with taking significant positions in a company and holding them, often for prolonged periods. If such an approach would make you lose sleep at night, you should scale back your expectations to returns of 10–20 per cent on a diversified portfolio.

Having fewer but more significant holdings flies in the face of the famous investment maxim, "don't put all of your eggs in one basket." Rather, it heeds another piece of wisdom, "put a significant number of your eggs in carefully held baskets, then keep track of the baskets."

Benjamin Graham, the father of value investing, is the more famous of the Buffett mentors. Yet he too spoke against diversification strictly for the sake of owning a "complete" portfolio of stocks.

Buffett's previous and current portfolios contain approximately ten stocks, which mirrors his stated feelings that with each investment that you make, you should have the courage and conviction to place at least 10 per cent of your net worth in that stock. Buffett's researched, patient approach ties in with the related goal of investing for the very long term, as once you find a good company you will want to hold it, often for periods of a decade or more. There are whole sectors of the economy, as well as types of investments, that Buffett has avoided entirely and never felt the need to purchase to pursue an elusive goal of "rounding out a diversified portfolio."

Diversification reduces your overall portfolio risk, and increases your overall probability of investment success, but it will also lessen the magnitude of this success. If you find a successful mutual fund you will notice that the fund is likely concentrated on several key sectors or stocks, but it is unlikely that it is invested in a diversified portfolio of securities.

Two

Home Sweet Home

The primary motivation for buying a home shouldn't be to make money. The price of a home, including yours, isn't likely to increase as quickly as many other investments. Still, while the easy money in real estate is likely over, it can still make prudent financial sense to purchase a home.

The 1980s were great years for real estate, and they sure were fun while they lasted. You bought a house—it didn't matter where, but Toronto or Vancouver were favourites. It also didn't really matter what type of house you got—large suburban bungalow, a new townhouse, or a tiny condo in the sky. You used as little of your own money as possible, thus getting the most financial leverage. You sat back and watched your home rise in value. You repeated, when necessary, with cottages, or condominiums where you never really worked too hard to rent them out. In many instances the rental return didn't matter—capital appreciation was the game.

The past decade has provided a number of lessons, primarily that real estate can go down as well as up. But it has also shown us the risks of financial leverage and that not all real estate is created equal—that you can have gluts of bachelor condominiums that few people actually want to purchase, and perhaps fewer wish to live in, at almost any price. At another level, this has shown us that not all geographic areas can sustain huge price increases.

It is important to remember that forecasts about the future of real estate prices are the same as predictions about stock prices or interest rates. Nobody can say for certain if there will be another bubble that would force unreasonable prices even higher. But why build your hopes around that, when you can undertake actions based on solid, reasonable, and more modest expectations to own your home?

Thus, the primary motivation for buying and owning a house should be to have a place to live, not to make money. When you purchase a home you have the ability to "lock in" your cost. You will know how much your monthly bill is, including gas, hydro, water, and mortgage. Over time this won't change drastically, and after 25 years or less you will have your house paid for. On the flip side of this is the comparison of rental costs vs. purchase carrying costs. The alternative to buying a home isn't not buying one, it is renting one. In some cases, the activity of the past decades and existing regulations have resulted in market inefficiencies where rental costs can be below comparable costs of home ownership. The choice is there.

The following chapter will deal with your home as an investment, how to shop for a good mortgage rate, how to use your RRSP to buy your first home, the comparison between paying down your mortgage or contributing to an RRSP, and the circumstances when you should consider a reverse mortgage.

Your Home—A Good Investment

Tip 12

WHILE THE RAPID APPRECIATION OF RESIDENTIAL REAL ESTATE OF PAST DECADES IS OVER, OWNING YOUR HOME CAN BE A WISE PURCHASE— DEPENDING ON THE CITY YOU LIVE IN, THE TYPE OF HOUSE YOU BUY, YOUR NEIGHBOURHOOD, YOUR ORIGINAL PURCHASE PRICE, INTEREST RATES, AND THE RENTAL MARKET. HOWEVER, THE LARGEST REASON FOR BUYING A HOME FOR MANY PEOPLE IS SOMETHING THAT YOU JUST CAN'T PUT A PRICE ON—THE DESIRE FOR HOME OWNERSHIP. ALL OTHER FACTORS THAT DETERMINE THE WORTH OF A HOUSE AS AN INVESTMENT ARE FINE, BUT IT IS WISE TO CONSIDER THAT REAL ESTATE BUBBLES WILL CONTINUE TO APPEAR IN THE FUTURE, AND RUNNING AFTER A FAST-RISING REAL ESTATE MARKET CAN BE A COSTLY GAME IN THE END.

You need a place to live. The opposite of buying a home isn't not buying one, it is renting. In some cases rental markets have shifted to the point where in the cold financial balance it makes sense to rent your accommodation. To see if this is true in your case, add up all of the annual costs of ownership: mortgage interest, taxes, maintenance, insurance, and all utilities, and subtract the amount that your mortgage is paid down in that year. Compare the resulting figure to the costs of renting a similar property.

Notice that this rough calculation leaves off any appreciation of the house itself, which is a tax-free gain. In addition, there are a few distinct advantageous to home ownership:

- Mortgage payments will not rise as quickly as rental rates.

- Unlike rental payments, you will eventually pay off the mortgage.

- Prices of homes have appreciated, generally speaking, over the long-term.

You should therefore approach an investment in your home like an investment in real estate by making comparisons with the other investment options available.

- If you are looking at real estate as an investment, think about how you can add value to the property, rather than letting inflation bail you out. Are you going to renovate the property, rezone to other uses, internalize the property management function by doing all of the work yourself, or all of the above?

- Don't be surprised if it is difficult to find a property that makes economic sense for you— in some locations and times standard methods of evaluating properties seem to go out the window (the condo market of the late 1980s for example).

Finally, if you insist on investing in additional real estate outside your home, consider Real Estate Investment Trusts (REITs), real estate stocks, or a real estate mutual fund, none of which will phone you in the middle of the night asking you to unplug the toilet. AGF, CIBC, Dynamic, and Mackenzie are all mutual fund companies that offer real estate mutual funds.

Shopping for the Best Mortgage

Tip 13

MOST CANADIANS LIVE IN ONE OF THE LARGEST INVESTMENTS THAT THEY WILL EVER MAKE. IT IS ALSO TRUE THAT MOST HOMEBUYERS REQUIRE A MORTGAGE TO FINANCE THEIR HOME AND THAT THE MORTGAGE IS THE LARGEST DEBT THAT THEY WILL EVER UNDERTAKE. TO MANY PEOPLE, THINKING ABOUT THE MORTGAGE MEANS ENSURING THAT THERE IS ENOUGH IN THE BUDGET TO MAKE THE NECESSARY MONTHLY PAYMENTS. THEY SHOULD ALSO TAKE THE TIME TO COMPARE A FEW INSTITUTIONS FOR THEIR MORTGAGE NEEDS.

Why bother to comparison shop for a mortgage? Many people will comparison shop for the little things, but broadly ignore larger items that matter the most. They will go to the cheaper gas bar and save 50 cents when they fill up the car, but when it comes to their mortgage they will pick up the phone and call one or two banks and accept the prevailing mortgage rate without negotiating. A difference of one tenth of 1 per cent on a mortgage can save you $100 per year on mortgage payments. It is hard to save an equivalent amount on your gasoline bill.

In reality, there is probably more competition between financial institutions in the mortgage field than in any other area. New and changing innovations also make straightforward comparisons difficult—it isn't like comparing GIC rates. Here are some guidelines:

- The old rule still applies: choose the shortest amortization period that you can afford. Increasing your monthly payments or repaying a portion of your mortgage by a few dollars can decrease the time it takes to repay your mortgage by up to 10 years. In turn, you save on interest payments.

- There are a huge variety of mortgages, including fixed rate, variable rate, and combination rates that can suit your needs and budget.

- Loyalty programs such as cash back packages are also available.

- You can make monthly (the most common), semi-monthly, biweekly, or weekly mortgage payments. The latter two will pay back your mortgage the fastest.

- The HomeCalculator software offered at www.b4usign.com allows you to make comparisons between different amortization schedules, interest costs, and payment periods in differing scenarios.

- The Internet makes timely comparisons between different banks, financial institutions, and credit unions much easier.

- Many financial institutions will guarantee an interest rate on a mortgage agreement ahead of time—often for a period of up to 90 days.

- Everything is open for negotiation: the rate that you will actually pay can depend on your existing business with the financial institution (accounts, credit cards, other loans), and the competitiveness of the market at the time. Bargain, and look for rates of up to 1/4 per cent off current posted rate levels.

In short, the mortgage bill is a big monthly expense—managing it accordingly could save you thousands of dollars.

RRSP Home Buyers' Plan

Tip 14

MANY YOUNG PEOPLE STRUGGLE TO FIND A JOB, PERHAPS PAY OFF STUDENT LOANS, AND MAKE CAR PAYMENTS. ONCE ALL THEIR BILLS ARE PAID THEY FREQUENTLY DON'T HAVE ENOUGH MONEY TO BUY THEIR FIRST HOUSE OR CONDO. TO ASSIST THE FIRST-TIME HOMEBUYER THE FEDERAL GOVERNMENT INTRODUCED THE HOME BUYERS' PLAN IN THE 1992 FEDERAL BUDGET. THE HOME BUYERS' PLAN WAS INTENDED TO BE A SHORT-TERM PROGRAM THAT WOULD ALLOW PEOPLE TO BORROW FROM THEIR RRSP TO PURCHASE A HOME TAX-FREE. SINCE THEN, ALMOST 650 000 CANADIANS HAVE WITHDRAWN OVER $6 BILLION TO FINANCE THE PURCHASE OF A HOME.

As with any program, there are rules to follow. Individuals who are Canadian residents can temporarily withdraw up to $20 000 from their RRSP to acquire a new home in Canada. There are no penalties, no interest charges that have to be paid, and no withholding taxes. A married couple or common law couple may withdraw a total of $40 000 between them. The home purchased must be in Canada and must be your first principal residence in Canada.

A few additional points should be considered.

- RRSP contributions made less than 90 days before being withdrawn are not eligible to be withdrawn.

- Individuals or their spouses cannot have occupied a principal residence during the previous four years.

- You must withdraw the money within 30 days of buying the home, and the completion date must be before October 1st of the year following.

Most importantly, the money that is withdrawn has to be repaid to the plan. Payments must be made in annual installments over a 15-year time frame commencing no later than 60 days after the end of the second year following the withdrawal. This is a minimum requirement; you can pay more than this at any time. Repayment must be made to an RRSP that you hold, but not necessarily the one that served as the original source of the funds. If you don't repay the loan the portion of the loan that was due becomes taxable income.

Is it worth it? The program allows you to pay your mortgage off faster, which is beneficial, since mortgage interest is paid with after-tax dollars. However, you will incur an opportunity cost, namely the loss of tax sheltered, compound growth of money within an RRSP. On the whole, the positives typically outweigh the negatives, but the decision should be made within the context of a complete financial plan.

Some of these disadvantages can be mitigated if the amount of money saved by having a lower mortgage is reinvested at a good rate of return. Investors should also seek to repay their withdrawn funds faster than the 15-year maximum, in order to return to having maximum opportunities for their RRSPs.

Any first-time homebuyer should seriously consider this program. It is a program with excellent flexibility that makes solid sense in most cases.

Do You Pay Down the Mortgage or Contribute to Your RRSP?

Tip 15

THE HOTTEST FINANCIAL QUESTION FOR MANY CANADIANS IS WHETHER TO PAY DOWN THE MORTGAGE OR MAKE AN RRSP CONTRIBUTION. THIS IS ONE OF THE MOST HIGHLY DEBATED QUESTIONS IN ALL OF PERSONAL FINANCE, AND IS MADE ALL THE MORE COMPLEX BECAUSE THERE IS NO CLEAR RIGHT OR WRONG ANSWER FOR ALL INVESTORS. IT COMES DOWN TO THE INVESTOR'S OWN PERSONAL DECISION AND VIEWS ON WHAT THE FUTURE BRINGS. HOWEVER, THERE ARE SEVERAL RULES OF THUMB THAT CAN BE APPLIED:

- You need to have unused RRSP contribution room. If you have maximized your RRSP contributions you won't be able to make any additional contributions.

- How close are you to retirement? People who are near retirement age should make their RRSP contributions.

- What is your marginal tax rate? The higher your marginal tax rate, the more advantageous is the RRSP contribution. Investors with higher marginal tax rates benefit more from RRSP contributions than do investors in a lower tax bracket. In addition, if you expect your marginal tax rate to be lower at retirement, make the RRSP contribution.

- How much do you owe on your mortgage and how long is your amortization schedule? Investors with a large mortgage and a long amortization schedule should pay down the mortgage and save the resulting interest expense. For example, if you have a $100 000 mortgage and your interest is 7 per cent per year, you will pay $212 033 on principal and interest over 25 years. However, if you contribute an additional $1000 to your principal payments within the first five years of your mortgage, you would save more than $2869 on interest payments during the next 20 years. At that time you can use the money for your RRSP contributions, a time that you will probably be in a higher tax bracket as well.

- Assess the current capital market environment. If prospects for GICs, mutual funds, and stocks (i.e., the investments that you would make in your RRSP) don't look good, take the sure thing and pay down the mortgage. Investing in an RRSP is only advantageous if you earn a higher rate of return in your RRSP than the interest you have to pay on your mortgage.

- Know your risk tolerance. If you are risk averse and if all of your RRSP investments are in fixed income investments, then pay down the mortgage.

- Determine your future income potential. If you expect to have a big raise, which will place you into a higher tax bracket, then pay down the mortgage and save the RRSP contribution room for later.

Remember that there is no single rule that applies in all cases, at all times. However, either one is a wise strategy, and beats spending the money or investing in the latest hot stock.

Consider a Reverse Mortgage…
as Your Last Option

Tip 16

HOMEBUYERS OFTEN SAVE RIGOROUSLY FOR THEIR HOME, FORGOING EXPEN-
DITURES AND MAKING SACRIFICES TO PAY DOWN THE MORTGAGE AND SAVE
FOR RETIREMENT. AT RETIREMENT THEY GET TO ENJOY THEIR DREAM HOME
DEBT-FREE. THE ONLY PROBLEM WITH THIS SCENARIO FOR A LOT OF RETIREES IS
THAT THEY LIVE ON A FIXED, AND OFTEN NOT VERY LARGE, INCOME.

One option is to take a reverse mortgage—a loan against the home, which brings you money while you still live in your home. You can usually borrow between 10 to 40 per cent of the value of your home depending on your age. A reverse mortgage loan requires no repayment for as long as you live in your home and you will never owe more than the value of your home.

This loan is different from a traditional mortgage in two ways. In order to qualify for a traditional mortgage, the bank checks your income to see how much you can afford to repay each month, but with a reverse mortgage there are no monthly repayments. With most loans, if you fail to make your repayments, you are in trouble. With a reverse mortgage you don't have any repayments. Thus, the debt grows larger as you keep getting cash advances and the interest is added to the amount you owe. This is why a reverse mortgage is called a "rising debt, falling equity" loan. As the amount you owe (your debt) grows larger, your equity (the value of your home less debt) is getting smaller.

You can receive income from your reverse mortgage in two ways. You can take the loan and invest it in an annuity. In turn, this annuity will provide you with income until your death. The second alternative is to receive monthly income from your reverse mortgage provider. Here you simply increase the size of your loan on a regular basis in order to receive income.

There is one big downside to all of this—you still owe money on your home. The total amount you will owe at the end of the loan will equal the loan plus all the interest accrued. All the interest can be a substantial amount of money.

Before you apply for a reverse mortgage, discuss your options with your family. Remember that a reverse mortgage will reduce the size of your final estate.

Three

The RRSP for You!

Stop! Read the following sentence slowly. Your Registered Retirement Savings Plan (RRSP) is your most important investment tool—period. First, if you make an RRSP contribution you can deduct your contribution from your taxable income. This is a large benefit because it saves you taxes today. Next, any investments in your RRSP are not taxable until you take the money out of the RRSP. Thus, you can switch, sell, and buy different investments in your RRSP without incurring any tax liabilities. Finally, when you retire you will theoretically also be in a lower tax bracket and thus will be able to pay less tax when you actually spend your money.

Many Canadians use the words investing and RRSP synonymously. And there is little doubt that an RRSP should serve as a cornerstone of your overall portfolio. But taking a step back from all of the hype, it is important to understand what RRSPs and investments are and how they are different, and therefore what they can and cannot do for you. First, your RRSP is not an investment, you still have to place your money in an investment. An RRSP is like a shoebox, it has no value, but you can place an investment in your RRSP (the box). When you make the contribution to your RRSP (place the money in the box) you get to claim a tax deduction (you save tax). Then the money in the box (in the RRSP) is not taxed while it is in the box. Only when you cash in the investments and take them out of your RRSP (out of the box) do you have to pay tax. In short, once in the box you still have to invest in something that has value (like a GIC or mutual fund). The value of the RRSP comes from the tax advantages, which in turn can increase your net worth and income.

At its most basic level, an RRSP allows you to defer taxes to a point later in your life, and allows tax-free compounding within the plan. Let's look at each of these points. The fact that this is a method of deferring, not eliminating taxes, is probably forgotten by some people in their rush to contribute early in the year so that they can get a tax refund when they make out their tax returns. But the point is still there: you are not paying taxes today (hence the tax refund), but will be paying taxes upon retirement, a point in the future when you will be, in all likelihood, at a lower marginal tax bracket. Putting off the payment of a tax is generally a good strategy, and many complex tax shelters are built around the premise of paying taxes tomorrow, rather than today.

However, there are some exceptions to this rule. Those who are near retirement age, and who have built up substantial RRSP assets, may find that further tax deferral is not in their best interest. They could conceivably be in the highest tax bracket at retirement, and may face clawbacks of entitlements due to the income they will be receiving from pensions, investments, and their RRSP.

The other aspect of RRSPs, which is tax-free compounding, is another powerful investment tool. As a simple example, take $10 000 and invest it in a GIC that earns 6 per cent, on which tax is paid annually. After 10 years, this would grow to a little over $14 000. The same amount of money, for the same time in an RRSP would grow to just under $18 000.

This is a significant difference, based on a relatively small amount of money invested for a period far shorter than the typical RRSP investment period.

Which brings up the final point—invest in your RRSP early. The earlier that you start your contributions to your RRSP, the longer your money can compound. Even relatively small amounts of money, compounding over 35 or more working years, will grow substantially. The strategy is to start early and continue every year that you can. Making contributions early means starting early in your working lifetime and making contributions early in the year. Many people make their contributions based on their last year's tax return—they contribute in the first days of the year 2000 to get a refund on their 1999 tax return. Such an approach loses out on a full year of compounding. Make your contributions for the past year, and add your money for this year as well. If you can't come up with the money all at once consider making monthly payments into your RRSP or applying for an RRSP loan— if capital market conditions are favourable borrowing to invest in an RRSP is very advantageous. Investors who have neglected to invest in their RRSP for several years could make one large RRSP contribution, save big taxes and repay the majority of their loan with the tax refund.

The following chapter highlights how to profit from an RRSP and outlines RRSP strategies. It will detail how a conventional RRSP and a self-directed RRSP differ, how to save money with a spousal RRSP, and how to benefit from transfers and contributions. We will also discuss various strategies for getting around the foreign content limits, how to hold a mortgage in your RRSP, and how to benefit from Registered Education Savings Plans.

Remember that your RRSP is the most important tool that you can use to achieve your investment objectives because it allows you to save big money in taxes while making the investments that you would normally make.

How to Profit from Your RRSP

Tip 17

ONE OF THE BEST WAYS TO DEFER PAYING TAX TODAY IS TO MAKE A REGISTERED RETIREMENT SAVINGS PLAN (RRSP) CONTRIBUTION. AN RRSP ALLOWS YOU TO CLAIM AN IMMEDIATE DOLLAR-FOR-DOLLAR TAX DEDUCTION, WHICH REDUCES YOUR TAXABLE INCOME. IN ADDITION, YOUR CONTRIBUTIONS CAN COMPOUND TAX-FREE.

Almost every year Ottawa tinkers with RRSP rules—one year RRSP contribution maximums increase, in other years the types of investments allowed change, and the list goes on. While there has been some tinkering of the rules in the most recent Federal Budgets, the basics haven't changed much in recent years, nor have the reasons for putting money into these tax-deferred investment vehicles. It's very important to have an RRSP, so here are some of the basic rules:

- You can contribute up to 18 per cent of your earned income, up to a maximum of $13 500, plus any carry forward of any unused contribution space from years past. If you are a member of a Registered Pension Plan at work, you must subtract your year's Pension Adjustment from the amount you can contribute. Your Notice of Assessment makes your contribution limits clear.

- You are subject to a penalty of one per cent a month on that part of your RRSP contribution that exceeds your lifetime over-contribution limit of $2000. Any over-contributions of up to $8000 that were made before February 27, 1995 must be used first in lieu of new contributions to reduce the over-contribution to $2000. If you did not contribute your maximum RRSP contribution in any year since 1991, you may carry forward this amount indefinitely, subject to the age restrictions.

- You may contribute for last year's tax year within the first 60 days of the following year.

- An official receipt must be filed along with your tax return in order to claim your deduction. Many financial institutions will supply instant receipts near the contribution deadline, but more typically receipts are mailed.

- Upon death, your RRSP assets will be included in your estate's holdings in the year of death, and taxed in the normal way. However, a tax-free transfer can be made to a spouse, if they are listed as the designated beneficiary of the plan.

- There is a long list of investments that are eligible to be held in an RRSP. They include Guaranteed Investment Certificates (GICs), term deposits, Canada Savings Bonds (CSBs), most bonds, stocks that trade on Canadian stock exchanges, and mutual funds that invest in these securities, just to name a few. Foreign investments are limited to 25 per cent (30 per cent in 2001) of the book value (the original cost) of your RRSP.

RRSPs are a wonderful tax deferral mechanism, and should be used by almost every investor. Establishing an RRSP is probably one of the most successful investment strategies that you will ever implement.

How to Profit from RRSP Strategies

Tip 18

JUST BECAUSE RRSPS ARE WIDELY USED AND PROBABLY USED BY YOU, DOESN'T MEAN THAT THEY ARE ALWAYS USED CORRECTLY OR THAT YOU CAN'T TWEAK YOUR STRATEGY A LITTLE FOR SOME BIG GAINS. HERE ARE SOME STRATEGIES THAT YOU MAY NOT HAVE THOUGHT OF TO MAKE AND SAVE YOU MONEY:

- RRSPs can be opened generally by anyone with earned income, and are not restricted by age. If a child has earned income he or she may have an RRSP and make RRSP contributions. You may contribute to an RRSP until the end of the year in which you turn 69.

- Remember that you can withdraw money at any time from your RRSP, which is then taxed at your current marginal rate. Such a strategy may make some sense at a time when you are at a lower tax bracket. For example, when you are pursuing an opportunity to return to school, or have taken a leave from the workforce to raise children you will pay taxes on the withdrawal, but likely at a lower rate.

- Make your contributions as early in the year as you can to benefit from a years' worth of tax-free growth rather than waiting for the first 60 days of the following year.

- Most investors should aim to maximize their contributions as much as possible. For many, this may be best achieved through a regular contribution program.

- Your RRSP is a long-term investment; most people will not be collapsing their RRSP for at least several decades. Equities and equity-based mutual funds are investments well suited for your RRSP.

- It is important for investors who own interest-bearing investments to first include these investments in their RRSP and hold their stocks outside their RRSP for tax reasons. It is much preferable to hold debt-based investments, such as strip bonds, within an RRSP as the interest on these investments can grow tax-free. Still, investors should realize that even after forgoing these benefits equities will still outperform fixed income securities over the long-term.

- Though there are a wide variety of investments that are allowed in an RRSP, there is little to be gained by pursuing more esoteric investments, or following shorter term trading based strategies. Capital losses cannot be used to offset any capital gains within an RRSP, and thus any losses incurred within a plan go straight to your bottom line.

The Self-Directed RRSP—
How It Can Work for You

Tip 19

IF YOU GO TO A GENERAL MOTORS DEALERSHIP YOU EXPECT TO SEE GM CARS,

ALTHOUGH IF YOU GO TO A USED CAR DEALERSHIP YOU EXPECT TO SEE CARS

FROM A VARIETY OF AUTOMAKERS. THE SAME SITUATION EXISTS WITH RRSPS. IN

A MANAGED OR CONVENTIONAL RRSP YOU WILL HOLD INVESTMENTS

PROVIDED BY THE FINANCIAL INSTITUTION THAT PROVIDES THE RRSP. INVESTING

WITH A SELF-DIRECTED RRSP IS LIKE GOING TO THE USED CAR DEALERSHIP IN

THAT IT GIVES YOU MORE CHOICE.

A conventional RRSP is usually established by a first-time investor or an investor who places their money in the investment products offered by one financial institution. This form of plan is popular for Canadians, and is chiefly sold through banks, life insurance agents, mutual fund companies, and financial planners. The advantage of a conventional RRSP is cost; any cost associated with such a plan is usually waived by the financial institution. The disadvantage is flexibility; you can only hold the investments that are offered by one financial institution. Thus, it is not possible to invest in one stock, a mutual fund, and a GIC in one account.

The biggest advantage of a self-directed RRSP is its ability to invest in a multiple number of investments from a variety of providers. You can place GICs and mutual funds in your self-directed RRSP, but you can also place stocks, bonds, and a full scope of qualified investments. With a self directed RRSP you have full control, and can shift around assets as you see fit. Such plans are typically associated with stock brokerages and investment dealers, but are also offered in various forms by banks, trust, and mutual fund companies. While there is a broad range of investments permitted in any RRSP, there may be limitations placed by the institution that holds your self-directed plan. For example, not all types of mutual funds from all families are available through some self-directed plans. Nonetheless, the options are considerably more than with a conventional RRSP.

The advantage of a self directed plan is the flexibility and control that you have over your own investments. Within the rules outlining qualified investments within RRSPs, you can pretty much hold any type of investment that you may wish to invest in. Some of the more esoteric investments, such as holding a mortgage on your home, can only be held in a self-directed plan. Management of such a plan is often easier than keeping track of many different investments plans scattered through different financial institutions. This ease of management is particularly important when calculating the full extent of foreign contribution limits, or when converting your RRSP into a RRIF. The cost associated with establishing an RRSP can be a few hundred dollars but you can negotiate if your assets are substantial. For investors with more than $20 000 to invest the cost is well worth the benefit.

How to Save with a Spousal RRSP

Tip 20

THERE ARE MANY MISCONCEPTIONS ABOUT SPOUSAL RRSPS. OPENING OR CONTRIBUTING TO SUCH A PLAN DOES NOT INCREASE THE AMOUNT THAT YOU OR YOUR SPOUSE CAN SHELTER IN AN RRSP. IT ALSO DOES NOT ALLOW FOR ANY INCREASED PAYOUT WHEN EITHER OF YOU RETIRE. BUT A SPOUSAL RRSP CAN SAVE YOU A LOT OF MONEY IN TAXES SINCE IT ALLOWS THE HIGHER INCOME EARNER TO CONTRIBUTE TO AN RRSP AND HAVE ALL THE WITHDRAWALS FROM THE RRSP GO TO THE SPOUSE.

Any contributions made to a spousal RRSP will belong to the spouse when withdrawn as either a lump sum or as a RRIF. The traditional use is for the partner who has a higher income, and thus a higher marginal tax rate, to set up a spousal RRSP for the spouse having a lower marginal rate. The higher income spouse claims the deduction because the deduction is more beneficial to the higher income earner. Upon retirement, the funds are then taxed in the hands of the lower income spouse, who presumably is at a lower marginal rate than the higher income spouse. This technique, like other income splitting tactics, is most effective when one spouse has little or no ongoing income.

If you and your spouse have two different marginal tax rates or have different amounts of money invested in RRSPs then a spousal RRSP is for you. In turn, if you and your spouse both have high marginal tax rates and both make RRSP contributions then a spousal RRSP will be of minor benefit. The idea is to have the same amount of money invested in each RRSP.

The mechanics are simple. An investor may give the unused portion of an annual RRSP contribution to his or her spouse. This contribution may be divided between the investor's RRSP and that of the spouse in any way that they wish, so long as the total allowable contribution is not exceeded. In addition, the spouse who receives the contribution does not have his or her own RRSP limits affected. The spouse who makes the contribution receives the associated tax deduction. You may also contribute to a spousal plan when you are past the age of 69 as long as your spouse is below that age limit.

There are a couple of things to watch for. A major tax liability may be incurred if a spousal plan is deregistered within three years of making the contribution. There are a few situations where withdrawals can be made without triggering any tax liability to the contributor. These include withdrawals when spouses are living apart due to marriage breakdown, when the contributing spouse dies, or when either of the two spouses become non-residents of Canada. Withdrawals made as part of the Home Buyer's Plan are also excluded. As well, there is no tax liability to the contributor if, when the plan matures and is either transferred into a RRIF or used to purchase an annuity, the withdrawals within the three-year period do not exceed the minimum amount specified.

Transfers and Contributions
Can Make You Money

Tip 21

MANAGING YOUR RRSP ISN'T LIMITED TO MAKING AN RRSP CONTRIBUTION, WHICH LEADS TO TWO ADDITIONAL POSSIBLE ACTIVITIES: TRANSFERS BETWEEN YOUR PLANS, AND CONTRIBUTIONS IN KIND.

TRANSFERS

In most cases, tax-free transfers may only occur between your own plans. Your contribution levels are not affected, no tax is payable, and there are no extra tax deductions.

Assets can be transferred from one RRSP plan to another. This is useful in cases where assets need to be rebalanced, or plans consolidated. Consolidating plans will allow you to better manage your investments prudently and increase your investment return without increasing your risk. Complete form T2033, available from either the Canada Customs and Revenue Agency or the institution to which you are transferring the assets, and be prepared for delays. Sometimes penalties are levied by the plan from which you are moving your money.

RRSP assets may only be transferred to your spouse in two ways. Upon marriage breakdown, funds from an RRSP may be transferred directly to the ex-spouse's RRSP or RRIF. The second type of transfer happens upon the death of the plan holder, when a tax-free transfer to a spouse or dependent child or grandchild is allowed if that person has been named as the beneficiary of the RRSP.

CONTRIBUTIONS IN KIND

Transfers should not be confused with contributions in kind, which use existing assets. Contributions in kind are utilized as the means of contribution to an RRSP without using cash. For example, assume that you are short of cash to contribute to your self-directed RRSP this year, but that you own shares of a mutual fund. Assume that this fund was bought for $7000, and has risen in value to $10 000. You can contribute these mutual fund shares directly to your plan at the market value of your units. This counts as an RRSP contribution and thus, in this example, qualifies for a corresponding tax deduction of $10 000.

Investors who have investments outside of their RRSP should consider a contribution in kind if they don't have the cash (and don't need their investments for short-term goals). The advantage is that you will be able to claim the tax deduction, get a tax refund, and keep your investment. In addition, you won't incur any transaction costs selling your investments and buying them back. The same approach can be used with a GIC that may be locked in for a period of time and could not otherwise be sold—simply make a contribution in kind to your plan.

While there has been no actual sale and repurchase of an investment, this transaction is treated as if a sale had taken place. Thus, in the above example, there was an implied capital gain of $3000. This gain must be declared, and as with any capital gain you will pay tax on two-thirds of the increase at your full marginal rate. In addition, your eligible RRSP contributions will decline by the amount of your transfer.

Getting Around
the Foreign Content Limits

Tip 22

WHILE WE LIVE, WORK, PLAY, AND INVEST IN CANADA, INVESTORS SHOULD ALSO LOOK AT MAXIMIZING THEIR EXPOSURE TO THE REST OF THE INVESTMENT WORLD. THE RULES HAVE RECENTLY BEEN LOOSENED, AND INVESTORS CAN NOW KEEP 25 PER CENT OF THEIR MONEY IN FOREIGN INVESTMENTS WITHIN THEIR RRSP. THIS MAXIMUM WILL RISE TO 30 PER CENT IN 2001.

- The primary motivation for investing outside of Canada is higher returns. During the past five years (ending December 1999) the best-performing equity market in the world was Finland, generating an average rate of return of 56.9 per cent per year. Canada generated a return of 20.9 per cent during the previous five years. While this was a good return, it was only the 9th best performing stock market in the developed world. The value of the Canadian stock market represents approximately 3 per cent of the world stock markets. Investors who ignore global investments are also ignoring 97 per cent of the investment opportunities available.

- Investors should go global because investing outside of Canada will reduce the risk in your portfolio. Global stock markets go up and down at different times than does the

Canadian stock market. By investing outside of Canada investors will ensure that their entire portfolio isn't subject to the same broader economic forces.

Investors who want to invest more than the allowed 25 per cent of their RRSP outside of Canada have three options. Each is different, and what is best for an investor will depend on particular circumstances.

- The first option is to invest in an RRSP-eligible mutual fund. These funds are also referred to as "clone" funds. They are called clone funds because they duplicate the performance of a foreign fund while remaining RRSP eligible. These RRSP-eligible funds invest in cash and forward contracts. This is the most attractive strategy to increase your foreign content exposure but it also the most expensive—it can cost as much as three per cent per year.

- The second option is to invest in an RRSP-eligible foreign fund. An RRSP–eligible foreign fund is different from a clone fund because it does not derive its value from another fund. These funds invest directly in options, futures, and forward contracts based on stock market indices, the remainder of the fund is invested in cash and thus the fund retains its RRSP eligibility. These funds are frequently index funds and charge "rock bottom" management fees.

- The third option is to invest in a Labour Sponsored Venture Capital Corporation (LSVCC). If you invest in one of these mutual funds the Canada Customs and Revenue Agency will allow you to increase your foreign content within your RRSP. For each $1 you invest in such a fund you will be able to increase your foreign investments by $3 to a maximum of 45 per cent of your RRSP (50 per cent in 2001).

For more information on global mutual funds, see Tip 37.

Holding Your Own
Home Mortgage in Your Plan

Tip 23

HAVE YOU EVER CONSIDERED BYPASSING THE TRADITIONAL ROUTE AND TAKING A MORTGAGE FROM YOURSELF—SPECIFICALLY THE HOLDINGS THAT YOU ALREADY HAVE IN YOUR RRSP? MORTGAGES, INCLUDING FIRST, SECOND, AND THIRD MORTGAGES, ARE ALL CONSIDERED RRSP ELIGIBLE BY THE CANADA CUSTOMS AND REVENUE AGENCY. IF YOU WANT TO INVEST IN A MORTGAGE WITHIN YOUR RRSP YOU CAN HOLD THE MORTGAGE ON YOUR OWN HOME—IN EFFECT TURNING YOUR PLAN INTO YOUR OWN MORTGAGE LENDER. THIS WILL ALLOW YOU TO FINANCE YOUR HOME PURCHASE AND PAY YOURSELF A HIGHER RATE OF INTEREST THAN THE RATE OF INTEREST THAT YOU MIGHT EARN FROM AN INSTRUMENT LIKE A GIC.

There are some rules, of course, that go along with this procedure. Non-arms-length mortgages, which usually refers to your own mortgage, but could also be a mortgage on a home held by an adult child, are permitted within an RRSP or RRIF, and in some provinces within a locked-in RRSP, also known as a LIRA. The interest paid cannot be less or more than what is offered by a standard financial institution, so you can neither use your RRSP as a source for cheap funds, or as a means of investing an excessive amount of money into your RRSP. Non-arms-length mortgages also must be insured by the Canada Mortgage and Housing Corporation (CMHC) or by G.E. Capital. This fee must be paid even if the mortgage would not otherwise have to be insured if a more typical mortgage were obtained. These fees are not insubstantial—they range from 0.5 per cent to 2.5 per cent of the mortgage loan. This insurance fee is a one-time cost, and can be added to the face value of the mortgage.

There is more. All of the fees associated with any mortgage application must also be paid with a mortgage held in your RRSP. This includes legal fees, appraisal fees, and initial application fees. This can add another $500–$1000 to the costs involved. And there are ongoing annual fees as well, which include the trustee fees of holding a self-directed RRSP, and an additional mortgage administration fee, each of which can add a couple of hundred dollars to your total. There is also all of the paperwork that goes into making any loan application.

While it is possible to do all of this, each investor has to question whether or not this is an appropriate investment to be held in their RRSP. The large fees associated with starting such a plan also make holding a small mortgage, say of only $25 000–$50 000, economically unfeasible. Holding a mortgage in your RRSP is only wise if the mortgage rate that you would pay is much higher than what you would otherwise earn in your RRSP investments.

Registered Education Savings Plan
and a 20 Per Cent Bonus

Tip 24

NOT TOO LONG AGO, REGISTERED EDUCATION SAVINGS PLANS (RESPS) EXISTED

ON THE FRINGES OF THE INVESTMENT WORLD. RESPS ARE PLANS THAT ARE

PRIMARILY DESIGNED TO HELP YOU SAVE MONEY FOR YOUR CHILDREN'S OR

GRANDCHILDREN'S EDUCATION. THESE PLANS WERE NOT VERY ATTRACTIVE

FOR THE AVERAGE PARENT OR GRANDPARENT SAVING FOR THEIR CHILD'S

EDUCATION BECAUSE THEY WERE VERY RESTRICTIVE.

However, the situation has changed recently, making RESPs much more appealing and an essential component in most financial plans. Annual contributions are now $4000 per child. Contributions must be made on a calendar year basis and there is a lifetime limit on contributions of $42 000 per child. Unlike an RRSP, a contributor may not deduct the contribution from his or her personal income. However, like an RRSP, investment dollars within the plan grow tax-free. An RESP may continue for 25 years from its date of inception. When the growth component is withdrawn from the plan, a student who is enrolled in a postsecondary institution must include that income in his or her income in the year it is removed (presumably this student will be at a very low tax rate). Alternatively, a contributor can also withdraw the capital plus the accumulated income if they go back to school although there will be an additional tax of 20 per cent. An additional option with certain restrictions is transferring the unused amount to an RRSP. The Canada Customs and Revenue Agency will also allow you to change the beneficiaries of the plan in most cases.

New definitions of what constitutes a postsecondary institution are now quite broad, and include almost any university, college, community college, or similar educational institution located either in Canada or anywhere in the world.

However, what truly makes RESPs appealing is the new Canadian Education Savings Grant (CESG). Here, the Federal government will add to annual contributions to an RESP to an annual maximum of $400 per child (the actual grant amount is 20 per cent of the first $2000 contributed annually to a child's RESP). This grant is payable to an RESP for a child who is age 17 or under. Grant payments are not made to the contributor, but directly to the RESP. In order to receive the grant, additional paperwork is required, which must include a Social Insurance Number (SIN) for the beneficiary. You can obtain the necessary forms for a SIN from your nearest Canada Employment Centre, which will take about a month or two to process.

RESPs can be set up through mutual fund companies or your financial institution. The range of applicable investments that can be held is quite broad, and includes fixed income, money market, or foreign or domestic mutual funds and securities.

Four

The Golden Years

Retirement is a time of many changes, both for yourself and your investments. You will have to determine what happens to the investments in your RRSP, reacquaint yourself with your company pension plan, become familiar with government programs that exist for seniors, and be aware of tax and investment changes that affect retirees.

But there are many things that stay much the same. All of the financial principles discussed in other sections of this book, from maintaining a balance to having proper diversification and watching your tax treatment remain constant. Your tax-deferred investments in you RRSP are still important, and have always been important to people as they age. Statistics Canada reports that the largest contributions to RRSPs are made by those aged 45 to 54. However, starting in your 60s you will be faced with the prospects of turning this pool of assets into an income stream to pay for your retirement. There is a range of options available, but with these options come choices that have to be made. These choices are, like many of those in the investment world, between keeping power in your own hands, or in the hands of others, and balancing control and flexibility with the need for certainty and guarantees.

Retirement is a major life stage, which requires that some changes be made to your financial planning, and updates have to be undertaken of some older plans. Here is what you should look at first:

Understand your retirement needs. Just as you have prepared a budget at other times of your life, sit down and prepare estimates of the amount of money you will need to fund your retirement. Be aware of both your short-term cash needs and your longer term needs. All of this is important as RRIFs and your investment savings should allow you to draw the cash necessary to meet your needs—but you must to make an accurate estimate in order to ensure you will not over-withdraw, and thus trigger some social payment clawbacks.

Understand what you will receive. Ensure that you know what the "three pillars" of the retirement system can pay you. The "three pillars" are Old Age Security, the Canada Pension Plan, and tax-assisted vehicles such as RRSPs. If you have any questions, ask your financial advisor or the appropriate Federal department, your financial institution, or your former or current employer.

Prepare the paperwork. Start assembling the paperwork you, or perhaps your family, will need. This includes past income tax returns, pension and CPP statements, financial and bank statements, life insurance policies, and anything else that is appropriate, including your will.

Update your will. Although a will is important to almost anybody no matter what their age, it is especially vital for retirees. Without a will your beneficiaries will encounter long delays fulfilling your wishes when passing your assets to the required beneficiaries. You need a will.

Keep up to date. Stay abreast of changes in government benefits programs and income tax changes that affect seniors. Also stay current on changes to the investment world, and how your investment portfolio is behaving.

Stay current with technology. Whether it is direct deposits of CPP cheques to U.S. banks for snowbirds, or methods to pay your bills either by phone or online, technology is making many options easier for seniors. Try to keep on top of what can add ease to your life, and save you money as well.

Look for and negotiate bargains. There are financial benefits to being a senior, including reduced fees on some bank accounts or financial service transactions, as well as some savings that can be negotiated on everything from GIC rates to loans. Ask for, and search these out.

Be aware of the potential for outliving your money. While seniors should take a more conservative approach to their investments, the typical retiree will have to ensure that their portfolio provides income for at least a couple of decades. If you switch to a portfolio comprised entirely of safe investments such as GICs you can take a big hit in foregone returns, affecting your ability to keep up with inflation and perhaps to fully fund your retirement in later years.

Don't fall prey to aggressive investments. Now is not the time to be lured into aggressive tax shelters, investments in areas where you have no previous experience, or other high risk/high return investments.

All of this new jargon and new paperwork can be overwhelming. It comes at a time of other personal changes in your life. It can be too easy to put aside some of these decisions, but as you know they will still have to be made. The best advice is to keep up with the paperwork, making it easy for both yourself and your spouse or your eventual estate. Keep up to date with what is changing in the government, taxation, pension, and retirement world. And whatever happens, keep managing your investment assets mostly as you have up until now, with an eye to a little more income and safety at the expense of some, but not all, growth. This can help make these years truly the golden ones.

The following chapter will deal with retirement, when you retire, what government money is available, what pension plans you may have, and how to effectively reduce the tax you pay at, and during, retirement.

When You and Your RRSP Mature

Tip 25

EVENTUALLY IT COMES TIME FOR YOUR RRSP TO END. REMEMBER THAT YOUR RRSP IS SIMPLY A POOL OF ASSETS, WHICH HAVE GROWN ON A TAX-DEFERRED BASIS. RETIREMENT IS THE APPROPRIATE TIME TO ACCESS THESE ASSETS, PRESUMABLY TO REPLACE THE EMPLOYMENT INCOME THAT YOU HAVE LOST. IF YOU PLAN WELL YOU SHOULD BE ABLE TO WITHDRAW THESE INVESTMENTS AT A LOWER MARGINAL TAX RATE THAN WHEN YOU WERE EMPLOYED.

You have two viable options when it comes to turning your RRSP assets into an income stream to help support your retirement.

1. You can use the money in the plan to purchase an annuity, which will provide you with an income until a certain age or until the end of your life. Getting the best rate on an annuity can be a major shopping experience—one source for information is found at www.cannex.com, which gives many up-to-the-minute comparisons.

   While there are many types of annuities, they suffer from three basic problems. The first is that, in return for guaranteed payments for the future you give up control over your assets. For many investors who are used to playing an active role in their investments, this may not be an attractive option. A second drawback is that annuities can provide little protection against inflation. The final problem comes from today's low interest rate environment, which has reduced the rates paid on everything from GICs to annuities. However, you do "lock-in" an income stream, which could be beneficial for a conservative investor.

2. A preferable option is to purchase a Registered Retirement Income Fund (RRIF). A RRIF is like the reverse of an RRSP, in that it invests your money while it pays you an annual amount, based on prescribed minimums that are set by Ottawa. A further advantage, other than flexibility over withdrawals, is that the investments that you hold in your RRSP are eligible, with rare exceptions, to be held in your RRIF. Thus, there is no need to sell and transfer investments when you approach retirement. RRIFs can also supply inflation protection in two ways: you can take out an ever-increasing amount from your RRIF if inflation demands it, and the types of assets that you hold in your RRIF, such as stocks and equity-based mutual funds, can offer inflation protection.

For most active investors, the flexibility and control offered by a RRIF make it the option of choice, while for the most conservative investors the security of an annuity makes it preferable.

Tip 26

THERE ARE TWO BASIC SOCIAL SECURITY PROGRAMS IN CANADA FOR SENIORS.

HERE IS WHAT YOU NEED TO KNOW ABOUT OLD AGE SECURITY (OAS) AND THE

CANADA PENSION PLAN (CPP).

OLD AGE SECURITY

Old Age Security (OAS) provides a monthly pension, which is indexed to inflation, to all Canadian residents starting at age 65. As of January 1, 2000 the maximum annual pension was raised from $4960 to $5050 annually. The full pension is earned if the individual has 40 years of residence between the age of 18 and retirement. For those with a lesser degree of residence, but more than a 10 years of residence, the pension is equal to 1/40 of the full benefits for each year of Canadian residence.

  Payments are taxable and subject to clawback for those earning over $53 215. Programs related to the OAS are the Guaranteed Income Supplement, which is also an income-based program, and the Spouse's Allowance for widows and widowers of OAS recipients.

CANADA PENSION PLAN

The Canada Pension Plan (CPP) and the very similar Quebec Pension Plan are contributory plans, based on contributions made over the individual's working life. Every person in Canada over the age of 18 who earns a salary must pay into the Canada Pension Plan. As of January 1, 2000, the maximum annual pension was raised to $9155 for the Canada Pension Plan (up from $9020). Individuals are eligible for benefits starting at age 65 or at age 60 if they are substantially retired (but they will receive a lower amount—six per cent less per year). There are three types of benefits: disability benefits, survivor benefits, and the more typical retirement pension.

Neither CPP payments nor OAS payments are automatic. You have to apply on forms obtained from your nearest Federal Health and Welfare Office, and to ensure prompt payment it is wise to apply a few months before you turn age 65.

The Canada Pension Plan keeps track of the contributions made over your earning lifetime. A Statement of Contributions is sent to people every four to five years, however, if you are nearing retirement it is important to ensure that your contributions have been recorded properly.

You can ask for a statement once a year. To receive your statement you can:

- Visit the Human Resources Development Canada web site at www.hrdc-drhc.gc.ca and download a request form. Address the mail to Contributor Information Management, Canada Pension Plan, 333 River Road, Vanier Ontario, K1A 0L1.

- Phone 1-800-277-9914.

The Statement will tell you what you have contributed, but more importantly will provide estimates of the benefits you will receive upon retirement. It is important to note that for those individuals many years away from retirement, these estimates may differ substantially from your final benefit, as they do not take into account any contributions in future years.

If you are at or near retirement, become familiar with these benefits, and adapt your financial plans accordingly.

Your Company Pension Plan

Tip 27

THE CANADIAN RETIREMENT INCOME SYSTEM IS OFTEN REFERRED TO AS A "THREE PILLAR" SYSTEM. THE FIRST PILLAR IS OLD AGE SECURITY (OAS), WHICH PROVIDES A BASIC INCOME FLOOR FOR ALL SENIORS. THE SECOND PILLAR IS THE CANADA PENSION PLAN (CPP), PROVIDING ADDITIONAL INCOME FOR THOSE WHO HAVE BEEN EMPLOYED. THE LAST PILLAR IS MADE FROM TAX-ASSISTED VEHICLES FOR INDIVIDUALS. THESE TAX-ASSISTED VEHICLES INCLUDE RRSPS AND OCCUPATIONAL PENSION PLANS. THE FOLLOWING WILL DISCUSS THE IMPORTANCE OF USING EACH PILLAR TO MAXIMIZE YOUR INCOME AT RETIREMENT.

The importance of your company pension plan can be illustrated by these two comparisons of the sources of income for low income and higher income seniors, obtained from Human Resources Development Canada for the year 1997. Low income seniors are seniors earning less than $12 500 per year. High income seniors are seniors earning more than $20 000 per year.

SOURCES OF INCOME FOR SENIORS

	LOW INCOME	HIGH INCOME
Source	Percentage of Income	Percentage of Income
CPP	17%	17%
OAS	70%	13%
Pension	3%	37%
Investment income	4%	15%
Other sources of investments	6%	18%

Clearly, higher income seniors receive more income from their pension plans and their investments. If you want to have a higher level of income at retirement, your investments and pension plan will play major roles.

There are two basic types of pension plans that your employer may have set up for you. The most common is the defined benefit plan, where the amount you receive in your monthly retirement cheque is specified. This is usually a function of both the number of years you have worked and your salary. Once vested, this benefit is guaranteed even if you leave your current source of employment. Formulas differ from plan to plan, and can either average your salary calculations or may be a flat rate based on length of employment. For details of your own plan, contact your employer's human resources department, or its pension administrator.

The other type of pension plan is a defined contribution plan, also known as a money purchase plan. In this case your final benefit is not defined; what is defined instead is how much money you and your employer contribute to a plan. Typically this is a fixed percentage of your income. Each plan participant has his or her own account, each of which will have differing amounts depending on the contributions and how the money has grown within the plan. In some plans employees have a major say in how this money is invested and can shift between types of investments according to their personal preference.

It is important for you to clearly understand any pensions that may be available to you. Talk to your employer's human resources department and make sure you understand what type of plan you have, and what you will be entitled to. And you should do it sooner rather than later, so that you can adjust the rest of your investment portfolio.

What Every Retired Person Should Know About Taxes

Tip 28

WHILE THE TAX BASICS REMAIN THE SAME FOR THOSE WHO ARE RETIRED, IN THAT INCOME STREAMS FROM VARIOUS SOURCES ARE TAXED IN THE SAME WAY NO MATTER WHAT AGE YOU ARE, THERE ARE A FEW THINGS THAT DIFFER FOR RETIREES WHEN IT COMES TO TAXES. AWARENESS OF THESE TAX MATTERS SHOULD MAKE AND SAVE YOU MONEY.

- RRSP deductions can be carried forward, thus some investors may find that they have deduction room even though they have retired. If this is the case, you may want to consider making contributions, which can be done until you are 69 years old in the year of the contribution.

- A major change for seniors that affects their cash flow is their responsibility to make their own tax installment payments. It is important to plan your RRIF withdrawals and the reporting of investment income in order to reduce your tax payments as much as possible.

- Seniors may be able to claim various tax credits and grants that are offered at the provincial level—be sure to check your tax return booklet for more information.

- Even if you are working, once you turn 70 you are no longer required to make contributions to the Canada Pension Plan (CPP). Lump sum CPP payments must be included in income in the year of receipt. CPP benefits may also be assigned to a spouse as a way to split income. Each spouse must be at least 60 years of age for the benefits to be split. Benefits can be split as a "single assignment" (one spouse receives CPP benefits and splits with a spouse who has made no CPP payments) or as a "double assignment" (both spouses can receive CPP benefits but the benefits are apportioned between them equally).

- Old Age Security (OAS) payments are reported as taxable income and are subject to clawback provisions for those with net incomes over the amount of $53 215. Splitting the CPP benefits may help avoid the clawback, as will the proper timing of sales of securities, which would trigger capital gains.

- Taxpayers are allowed to roll over into their RRSP a portion of their retiring allowance, if they receive a retiring allowance from their employer. Check with your employer if you qualify and for details.

- There are five personal payments (received from the government) that may be transferred between spouses. These include the pension income amount of $1000 or the amount of eligible pension income, whichever is less. The age amount is available to those 65 years of age and older. This payment starts at $3482 for those with a net income under $25 921 and is reduced to zero for those with incomes of $49 134 or more. The last three personal amounts that may be transferred between spouses include the disability amount, the education amount, and the tuition amount.

Knowing how your tax situation will change upon retirement is the first step of making the right financial decisions.

Five

Making Money with Your Mutual Funds

A mutual fund is quite straightforward. It invests in cash, bonds, stocks, or other securities and is managed by a mutual fund company. When you invest in a mutual fund, your investment is combined with investments from other mutual fund investors who also want to invest in the same fund. This large pool of investments is then managed by a professional who has the training and expertise to manage the mutual fund prudently. In short, a mutual fund is an investment that allows investors to pool their investments under the talents of an investment manager.

Mutual funds offer investors many benefits, such as diversification, professional management, low initial investments, ease of purchase and redemption, and higher returns. In turn, the mutual fund industry has expanded steadily through the past decades. Investors can also choose from a multitude of funds to meet a specific investment objective. A description of some major fund categories follows.

- Money market funds invest in short-term money market instruments. These short-term investments are very safe and these funds incur little risk. These investments are suitable for the most conservative investors.

- Canadian bond funds invest in bonds issued by the Canadian government, provinces, or corporations. These funds pay interest on a regular basis and are considered to be safe, though bond prices do fluctuate in value. These funds are appropriate for investors who require safety and income.

- Canadian balanced funds invest in a combination of securities that include cash, bonds, and stocks. These funds are appropriate for investors that require income and capital preservation.

- Canadian equity funds invest in Canadian companies traded on a Canadian stock exchange. These companies include BCE, Nortel, Seagram, TD Bank, CIBC, and the Royal Bank, among others. These funds are appropriate for investors who require growth and can withstand risk.

- U.S. equity funds invest in the largest stock market in the world—the United States. These funds invest in companies like Microsoft, Cisco, General Electric, and Intel. These funds are appropriate for investors who require growth and can withstand risk.

- International equity funds invest in companies located in countries throughout the world. These funds invest in Europe, Asia, the Far East, Australia, and to a lesser extent South America.

- Global equity funds invest throughout the world. These funds are an excellent starting point for a well-diversified investment portfolio.

However, mutual funds bring a few disadvantages as well:

- The fees charged by fund managers reduce a fund's total return.

- The individual investor has no influence over the specific investments selected by a fund manager.

- The flip side of diversification means that one investment held in a fund may perform well, yet another may perform poorly, so the investor never enjoys the full benefit of a single good investment (of course, the mutual-fund investor never suffers the full impact of a single bad investment, either).

- Mutual funds are not guaranteed, and investors can lose money if they buy when the fund price is high and sell when it is low.

Canadians have now invested more than $385 billion in mutual funds, and there are more than 2843 funds currently operating in Canada. Not only are more people than ever investing in mutual funds, but there are also more mutual fund products and investment alternatives to choose from. In addition, each year the mutual fund industry continues to offer investors new and innovative mutual funds. This has included segregated funds, protected funds, and mutual funds that are able to invest globally but retain their RRSP eligibility. All these developments will ensure that investors continue to have more choice and improve their risk and reward profile.

Once you have identified some mutual funds, you should then determine your investment objectives and tolerance for risk. Selecting the funds that correspond to your objectives and risk tolerance, you should then gather as much information about these funds as you can. You can find a lot of information in daily newspapers, magazines, and business journals as well as the Internet.

Finally, you should obtain prospectuses for funds of interest to you. The prospectus describes a mutual fund's investment objectives, the fees that it charges, and the risks associated with purchasing the mutual fund. The prospectus also includes the fund's most recent financial statements. You can order a copy of a fund's prospectus directly from the mutual fund company. You may also get a copy from your financial advisor.

Mutual funds are bought and sold through a number of channels, including:

Financial planners. Investors should realize that all financial planners cannot sell all mutual funds. Although he or she may sell a variety of mutual funds, a planner may also work for one particular fund company and restrict recommendations to that company's funds. You should ask a financial planner at the outset what limitations there are on his or her access to funds.

Stockbrokers. Employed by investment dealers, stockbrokers sell a wide range of mutual funds. They usually charge a commission for each transaction they conduct on your behalf. They can also provide you with a wealth of information and guidance on investing.

Discount brokers. These organizations charge lower fees than conventional stock brokers, but provide little or no guidance or information about particular investments.

Banks, trust companies, credit unions, and caisses populaires. Your local financial institution sells a variety of mutual funds, including its own.

Insurance salespersons. Your insurance representative usually sells mutual funds on behalf of his or her employer.

Buying direct. Many mutual fund companies sell directly to the public.

You can sell your mutual fund investments within two or three business days through the outlet where you purchased them. You may choose to sell your entire investment, or you can choose to sell units in smaller amounts. One popular method is to redeem your units through regular withdrawal plans that allow weekly, monthly, or quarterly withdrawals.

The following chapter will highlight some tips and answer some common questions about mutual funds, while dispelling some myths about this popular form of investing. We will cover the importance of management fees and loads, how index funds perform, how to protect yourself, what not to do, how to avoid unfavourable distributions, how to get around foreign content limits, and how to buy mutual funds on sale.

Look for Mutual Funds with a Low Management Expense Ratio

Tip 29

ASIDE FROM THE LOAD/NO LOAD DIFFERENCE BETWEEN MUTUAL FUNDS (SEE TIP 30), NOT EVERY MUTUAL FUND CHARGES YOU THE SAME ONGOING FEES. MUTUAL FUND COMPANIES ALSO MAKE MONEY ON YOUR INVESTMENTS BY CHARGING A MANAGEMENT FEE FOR LOOKING AFTER THE MUTUAL FUND. THIS FEE IS DEDUCTED FROM THE FUND'S RATE OF RETURN. THE MANAGEMENT FEE COVERS SUCH COSTS AS SUPERVISING THE FUND'S DAY-TO-DAY ADMINISTRATION AND OPERATIONS, THE MARKETING OF THE FUND, SALARIES, ACCOUNTING AND LEGAL FEES, AND DISTRIBUTION COSTS ASSOCIATED WITH THE FUND. THE TOTAL COST OF ALL THESE FEES IS CALLED THE MANAGEMENT EXPENSE RATIO (MER) OF THE FUND. THE MER HAS TO BE DISCLOSED IN THE FUND'S PROSPECTUS ON AN ANNUAL BASIS.

The MER is deducted from the total returns earned by the fund. Thus the returns marketed by all the mutual fund companies each RRSP season are after the deduction (or net) of the management expense ratio. Investors should pay attention to the MER because it is a cost that they are paying indirectly. For example, assume there are two funds that both generated a return of 12 per cent per year before fees. Fund A has a management expense ratio of 2 per cent while fund B has a management expense ratio of 1 per cent. After deducting the Management Expense Ratio, Fund A generated a return of 10 per cent while Fund B generated a return of 11 per cent. This 1 per cent adds up over time. Consider Jack who invested $1000 in fund A and Jill who invested $1000 in fund B. In ten years, Jack's investment is worth $2593.74 and he paid a total of $318.75 in management expenses. In ten years Jill's investment is worth $2839.42 and she paid a total $167.22 in management expenses. Thus, Jill will have an additional $245.68, or 9.47 per cent, in her investment account because she paid $151.53 less in management expenses during a 10-year time frame.

A good mutual fund manager will easily add value to his or her mutual fund that can easily justify a higher management fee, but this doesn't mean that you should ignore the management expense ratio for a fund. The table below illustrates the average perform-ance of various mutual funds during a 10-year time frame. Each investment category was broken into four quartiles based on Management Expense Ratios. For example, during the previous 10 years, the average rate of return for the Canadian bond funds with the lowest MER was 9 per cent. The funds with the lowest management expense ratios on average have also generated higher rates of return.

AVERAGE PERFORMANCE OF MUTUAL FUNDS

Quartiles	CANADIAN BONDS 10-Year Return	CANADIAN EQUITY 10-Year Return	U.S. EQUITY 10-Year Return
Lowest MER	9.0%	10.5%	17.2%
	8.3%	10.2%	16.1%
	8.1%	9.4%	15.7%
Highest MER	7.8%	9.9%	13.8%

This is something worth remembering when choosing a fund.

To Load or Not to Load? That Is the Question

Tip 30

MUTUAL FUND COMPANIES MAKE MONEY ON YOUR INVESTMENTS IN SEVERAL WAYS. FIRST, SOME MUTUAL FUND COMPANIES CHARGE AN ACCOUNT SET-UP FEE WHEN YOU WANT TO OPEN AN ACCOUNT, ALTHOUGH MANY WILL WAIVE THE FEE IF YOU ASK. SOME MUTUAL FUNDS ALSO CHARGE A SALES COMMIS-SION WHEN INVESTORS PURCHASE OR SELL UNITS IN THE FUND. THESE MUTUAL FUNDS ARE REFERRED TO AS LOAD FUNDS. A MUTUAL FUND COMPANY WILL ALSO CHARGE A MANAGEMENT FEE FOR MANAGING THE MUTUAL FUND, WHICH IS DEDUCTED FROM THE FUND'S RATE OF RETURN.

Knowing what you're paying for is very important because each option will entail different sales commissions and different levels of advice. This can have direct implications on your short and long-term investment returns and the ultimate success of your investment plan.

There are two types of load mutual funds. With a front-end-load fund, investors pay a commission ranging from 2 to 9 per cent every time they invest in a mutual fund. In return they usually pay no commission for selling the fund. The second type is a back-end-load fund, where the entire initial investment goes to work in the mutual fund. Investors pay no direct sales commission initially, but must leave their investment in the mutual fund for a minimum period. If they do not comply with this minimum period they will incur a redemption charge. The longer an investor has invested in the fund; the lower the redemption charge. Most redemption fees decline to zero after seven years. No load funds charge no fees for either investing in or selling your funds. It is important to remember that fees reduce returns.

All funds, including no load funds, still charge a management fee to the fund for managing the fund. Thus, the biggest difference between a load and no-load fund is the investor's ability to buy and sell units in the fund without incurring any selling commissions. Thus, all else being equal, investors should invest in no-load funds. However, all else is not equal. A quantitative analysis of investor behaviour that was conducted by DALBAR Financial Services in 1997 concluded that investors who work with an advisor and pay him or her a fee earn a higher long-term return.

Investors who are not knowledgeable about investments should use a financial advisor. The planner will also offer support and advice on portfolio construction, understanding risk, and related tax and estate matters. These investors should consider load funds to add a financial disincentive to switching investments. Investors who do not need advice should consider a no-load fund or investing in load funds through a discount broker at a lower commission. No-load investors should remember that they get what they pay for—a fund that they want, with no help attached.

The Reality of Index Funds

Tip 31

MOST MUTUAL FUNDS ARE CONSIDERED TO BE ACTIVE INVESTMENTS: THE PORTFOLIO MANAGER MAKES INVESTMENT DECISIONS AND IS EXPECTED TO ADD VALUE BY OUTPERFORMING AN INDEX THAT REPRESENTS THE PERFORM-ANCE OF THE STOCK MARKET. AN INDEX FUND IS A MUTUAL FUND THAT IS NOT ACTIVELY MANAGED. IT AIMS TO DUPLICATE THE PERFORMANCE OF THE MARKET BY MIRRORING THE COMPOSITION OF A MARKET INDEX. FOR EXAMPLE, A CANADIAN EQUITY FUND WILL ATTEMPT TO DUPLICATE THE PERFORMANCE OF THE TSE 300 INDEX—WHICH IS AN INDEX THAT MEASURES THE PERFORM-ANCE OF 300 DIFFERENT CANADIAN COMPANIES.

ADVANTAGES

The reason why index funds have become popular is because they have generated excellent returns compared to other mutual funds. They also have lower management expense ratios. Most worldwide indices have generated 1st quartile performances during the previous five years—this means that a fund investing in that index has generated a return greater than

75 per cent of funds during this time period. The columns on the right of the chart below disclose the relative performance of each index for each calendar year during that 5-year time frame.

INDEX FUND PERFORMANCE RANKING

FUND NAME	ANNUALIZED 5-YEAR RETURN	QUARTILE RETURN 1999	QUARTILE RETURN 1998	QUARTILE RETURN 1997	QUARTILE RETURN 1996	QUARTILE RETURN 1995
MSCI World Price	1	2	1	1	3	2
Nesbitt Burns Small Cap	3	2	4	4	1	2
S&P TSE 60	1	1	3	1	1	2
Salomon Asia Pacific	4	1	1	4	4	4
Salomon Europe Equity	1	2	1	1	1	1
Salomon Japan Equity	4	1	1	4	4	4
Salomon World Equity	1	2	1	1	2	1
TSE 300	1	1	3	2	1	2

Source: MorningStar Canada

The above table illustrates some very important concepts. First, index funds have added value during this time period. Over the long term, index funds generate better returns in more developed markets such as the United States.

DISADVANTAGES

Over time active funds have the ability to limit downside risk, since the managers can avoid poorly performing investments. Index funds don't have this ability; they mirror the market by tracking the index. The table above shows that index funds tend to be either first or last in terms of performance: there seems to be no middle ground. During the previous 10 years, an index that invests in bonds and stocks outperformed (not adjusted for fees) 65 out of the 84 Canadian balanced mutual funds that have a 10-year track record. This fact would make many investors invest in such an index fund, but investors should also note that such an index exhibited more risk than 58 out of the 84 Canadian balanced mutual funds. In addition, some mutual funds have the ability to generate very high rates of return—outperforming the index by up to 30 per cent.

Investors who are able to select good funds and who don't want to settle for average returns should focus on active funds. Investors who want an average return (which is better than most active funds), should consider an index fund.

Protect Yourself with Segregated Funds

Tip 32

SEGREGATED FUNDS WERE INITIALLY DEVELOPED BY THE INSURANCE INDUSTRY TO COMPETE AGAINST MUTUAL FUNDS. TODAY, MANY MUTUAL FUND COMPANIES ARE IN PARTNERSHIP WITH INSURANCE COMPANIES TO OFFER SEGREGATED FUNDS TO INVESTORS. SEGREGATED FUNDS OFFER SOME UNIQUE BENEFITS NOT AVAILABLE TO MUTUAL FUND INVESTORS.

Segregated funds offer the following major benefits that are not offered by the traditional mutual fund.

- Segregated funds offer a guarantee of principal upon maturity of the fund or upon the death of the investor. Thus, there is a 100 per cent guarantee on the investment at maturity or death (this may differ for some funds), minus any withdrawals and management fees—even if the market value of the investment has declined. Most segregated funds have a maturity of 10 years after your initial investment

- Segregated funds offer creditor protection. If you go bankrupt, creditors cannot access your segregated fund.

- Segregated funds avoid estate probate fees upon the death of the investor.

- Segregated funds have a "freeze option" allowing investors to lock in investment gains and thereby increase their investment guarantee. This can be a powerful strategy during volatile capital markets.

Segregated funds also offer the following less important benefits:

- Segregated funds issue a T3 tax slip each year-end, which reports all gains or losses from purchases and redemptions that were made by the investor. This makes calculating your taxes very easy.

- Segregated funds can serve as an "in trust account," which is useful if you wish to give money to minor children, but with some strings attached.

- Segregated funds allocate their annual distributions on the basis of how long an investor has invested in the fund during the year, not on the basis of the number of units outstanding. With mutual funds, an investor can invest in November and immediately incur a large tax bill when a capital gain distribution is declared at year-end.

There has been a lot of marketing and publicity surrounding segregated funds and how much value should be placed on their guarantee of principle protection. In the entire mutual fund universe, there have been only three very aggressive and specialized funds that lost money during any 10-year period since 1980. Thus, the odds of losing money after ten years are extremely low. If you decide you need a guarantee, it can cost as much as 1/2 per cent per year in additional fees.

However, with further market volatility these guarantees could be very worthwhile. Several good life insurance companies that you could consider include Clarica, Royal & SunAlliance, and Transamerica. In addition, most major mutual fund companies such as C.I. Mutual Funds, Mackenzie, Talvest, Templeton, and Trimark also offer segregated funds.

Lemmings and the Mutual Fund Investor

Tip 33

IF YOU ARE A DIEHARD SPORTS FAN YOU ARE LOYAL THROUGH THICK AND THIN. IF YOU AREN'T A BIG FAN YOU TEND TO JUMP ON THE BANDWAGON ONLY NEAR THE END OF A SUCCESSFUL SEASON. SOME INVESTORS EMPLOY THE LATTER STRATEGY WHEN IT COMES TO SELECTING THEIR FAVOURITE MUTUAL FUNDS. THESE INVESTORS FIND THE HOT TREND AND SIGN UP, BECAUSE IN THE SHORT-TERM THINGS SEEM TO BE PRETTY GOOD. UNFORTUNATELY, SELECTING GOOD MUTUAL FUNDS IS NOT AS EASY A SELECT-ING YOUR FAVOURITE TEAM IN THE SUPER BOWL. FIRST YOU HAVE MORE THAN TWO PICKS—WITH FUNDS YOU HAVE 2843 CHOICES—AND YOU HAVE TO MAKE A SELECTION THAT WORKS NOT ONLY ON SUPER BOWL SUNDAY BUT ON EVERY OTHER DAY OF THE YEAR AS WELL.

One of the most common ways of selecting a mutual fund is to invest with the crowd in today's hot funds. Unfortunately, jumping from one winning fund to another is a recipe for disaster. The mutual funds that the crowd follows typically have had a hot recent performance and tend to gather all the new mutual fund sales.

Investors as a whole are primarily allocating their new investments to a small number of mutual funds and to a smaller number of mutual fund companies. Investors have invested over $400 billion in the 2843 different mutual funds, but one-third of those assets are invested in only 50 of those funds and one-half of those assets are invested in the largest 100 funds.

There are benefits to following the market leaders. Larger mutual fund companies and larger funds have the ability to reduce costs and attract the best professional money managers. However, the biggest limitation is that today's best-selling mutual fund may not be tomorrow's winner. This is true for any mutual fund but it seems to plague the best seller, and the one that garners the most attention, the most often. For example, in 1997 the AIC Advantage Fund II was the best-selling mutual fund during that year. Since then the fund has generated a loss during the following two years while the average fund posted a gain.

So buying the Canadian equity fund that was yesterday's best-seller isn't a strategy that produces excellent returns. You do not have to go fully in the opposite direction and ignore these hot funds, but you should understand their limitations and strengths. They became best-selling funds because they have merit, but you have to assess that merit within your own well-diversified portfolio, and not the crowd's current investment trend.

Chasing Hot Funds

Tip 34

INVESTORS FREQUENTLY INVEST IN A FUND THAT HAS GENERATED ABOVE-AVERAGE PERFORMANCE DURING THE PREVIOUS YEAR. IN FACT, THE SINGLE BIGGEST CONTRIBUTING FACTOR TO NEW MONEY FLOWING INTO A MUTUAL FUND IS THE FUND'S SUPERIOR PERFORMANCE DURING THE PREVIOUS YEAR. THUS, INVESTORS TEND TO INVEST A LOT OF NEW MONEY INTO MUTUAL FUNDS THAT HAVE DONE WELL RECENTLY. MORE SPECIFICALLY, INVESTORS LIKE TO GO WITH MUTUAL FUNDS THAT HAVE GENERATED A RETURN HIGHER THAN 75 PER CENT OF SIMILAR FUNDS; THESE FUNDS ARE 1ST QUARTILE FUNDS.

With over 80 per cent of new mutual fund sales being invested in 1st quartile funds, it would be useful to examine how well these funds performed in subsequent periods. We looked at the consistency of performance for Canadian equity funds over the past 10 years. The table below illustrates the results. In 1990 there were 20 Canadian equity funds that were 1st quartile and in 1991, 4 of these 20 funds were still in the same 1st quartile. In 1998 there were 46 funds that were 1st quartile and in 1999, 15 remained first quartile. On average 32 per cent of 1st quartile funds remained 1st quartile the following year.

CONSISTENCY OF PERFORMANCE

YEAR	NO. OF 1ST QUARTILE FUNDS	YEAR	NO. STILL 1ST QUARTILE FUNDS	PERCENTAGE STILL 1ST QUARTILE
1999	63	2000	?	
1998	46	1999	15	33%
1997	37	1998	13	35%
1996	31	1997	14	45%
1995	29	1996	10	34%
1994	26	1995	6	23%
1993	24	1994	5	21%
1992	22	1993	9	41%
1991	21	1992	8	38%
1990	20	1991	4	20%

These results show that winners don't stay winners for long—sometimes up to 75% of the funds that were 1st quartile in one year had disappeared from that top category the next year.

The next step is to determine where 1st quartile funds come from—how did they perform before they became "winners"? The table below illustrates that in 1999 there were 63 1st quartile Canadian equity funds. In 1998, 15 of these funds were also 1st quartile, 7 of these funds were 2nd quartile, 7 were 3rd quartile, 17 were 4th quartile, and 17 were new funds.

IMMEDIATE HISTORY OF 1ST QUARTILE FUNDS

	1999	1998
1st Quartile	63	15
2nd Quartile		7
3rd Quartile		7
4th Quartile		17
New Fund		17

Therefore, investors should not ignore funds that have been out of favour recently, nor should they ignore new funds. Build a good diversified portfolio of mutual funds, but don't build a portfolio of funds that were yesterday's winners and expect that each fund will retain its winning status. It is the future that counts.

Market Timing with Your Mutual Funds

Tip 35

WHEN INVESTING IN BONDS, STOCKS, OR MUTUAL FUNDS, INVESTORS HAVE THE OPPORTUNITY TO INCREASE THEIR RATE OF RETURN BY TIMING THE MARKET—INVESTING WHEN STOCK MARKETS GO UP AND SELLING BEFORE THEY DECLINE. A GOOD INVESTOR CAN EITHER TIME THE MARKET PRUDENTLY, SELECT A GOOD INVESTMENT, OR EMPLOY A COMBINATION OF BOTH TO INCREASE HIS OR HER RATE OF RETURN. HOWEVER, ANY ATTEMPT TO INCREASE YOUR RATE OF RETURN BY TIMING THE MARKET ENTAILS HIGHER RISK. INVESTORS WHO ACTIVELY TRY TO TIME THE MARKET SHOULD REALIZE THAT SOMETIMES THE UNEXPECTED DOES HAPPEN AND THEY COULD LOSE MONEY OR FORGO AN EXCELLENT RETURN.

Timing the market is difficult. To be successful, you have to make two investment decisions correctly: one to sell and one to buy. If you get either wrong in the short term you are out of luck. In addition, investors should realize that:

- Stock markets go up more often than they go down.

- When stock markets decline they tend to decline very quickly. That is, short-term losses are more severe than short-term gains.

- The bulk of the gains posted by the stock market are posted in a very short time. In short, if you miss one or two good days in the stock market you will forgo the bulk of the gains.

Not many investors are good timers. *The Portable Pension Fiduciary*, by John H. Ilkiw, noted the results of a comprehensive study of institutional investors, such as mutual fund and pension fund managers. The study concluded that the median money manager added some value by selecting investments that outperform the market. The best money managers added more than 2 per cent per year due to stock selection. However the median money manager lost value by timing the market. Thus, investors should realize that marketing timing can add value but that there are better strategies that increase returns over the long-term, incur less risk, and have a higher probability of success.

One of the reasons why it is so difficult to time correctly is due to the difficulty of removing emotion from your investment decision. Investors who invest on emotion tend to overreact: they invest when prices are high and sell when prices are low. Professional money managers, who can remove emotion from their investment decisions, can add value by timing their investments correctly, but the bulk of their excess rates of return are still generated through security selection and other investment strategies. Investors who want to increase their rate of return through market timing should consider a good Tactical Asset Allocation (T.A.A.) fund. These funds aim to add value by changing the investment mix between cash, bonds, and stocks following strict protocols and models, rather than emotion-based market timing.

Unfavourable Distributions and Free Redemptions

Tip 36

THE 10 PER CENT REDEMPTION

Sometimes investors need to sell some of their mutual fund investments to finance a short-term emergency or to meet other needs. However, if they invested in a load mutual fund without paying a front-end commission they will have to pay a commission when they redeem shares in that fund. But there is an option to avoid paying a commission: it's called the 10 per cent free redemption.

When investors invest in a load mutual fund with a deferred sales charge they will pay no sales charge at the time of investment. However, a redemption charge will apply to any investment redeemed within six years of this initial investment. This redemption charge is applicable to the value of the investment when they are redeemed or the value of their original investment (depending on the company you deal with). The following table outlines how the redemption charge is calculated:

SAMPLE REDEMPTION CHARGES

IF AN INVESTOR SELLS UNITS OF A FUND, THEY WILL HAVE TO PAY A CHARGE OF*:	
During the first year	6.0%
During the second year	5.5%
During the third year	5.0%
During the fourth year	4.5%
During the fifth year	3.0%
During the sixth year	1.5%
Thereafter	0.0%

These rates will vary among mutual fund companies.

Investors who redeem a portion of their investment within six years can utilize the 10 per cent free redemption option. With this option, an investor can redeem 10 per cent of their investments in a given year without paying a redemption charge.

AVOIDING UNFAVOURABLE DISTRIBUTIONS

Investors who invest in mutual funds at the end of a year when a mutual fund increased sharply in value could end up receiving a large taxable distribution even if they haven't made any money. When mutual funds earn money they declare a dividend. Mutual funds have to declare annual distributions based on the number of shares or units outstanding, not based on how long an investor has invested in the fund during the year. With mutual funds, an investor can invest in November and immediately incur a large tax bill when the capital gains distribution is declared at year-end.

Investors have several options to avoid a big hit. They can redeem the investment before the distribution is declared, but they will probably pay their own capital gains tax on the appreciation of their mutual fund shares. If you're investing at the end of the year, you should call or contact your mutual fund company in the first week of December and ask for an estimate of any capital gains made by the fund, which will be distributed before the end of the year. If it's big, don't invest. The downside to this strategy is that you may miss a good investment. An alternative is to invest in a segregated fund (see Tip 32), which declares its distribution based on how long you have invested in the fund.

Going Global Through Mutual Funds

Tip 37

THERE ARE MORE THAN 13 500 DIFFERENT PUBLICLY TRADED COMPANIES IN THE WORLD TODAY, AND THERE ARE OVER 700 MORE COMPANIES EXPECTED TO GO PUBLIC WITHIN A YEAR. IN ADDITION, EVERY MAJOR DEVELOPED COUNTRY OFFERS INVESTORS VARIOUS BONDS TO INVEST IN. ALL OF THIS MAKES FOR A LOT OF DIFFERENT INVESTMENTS AND PLENTY OF CHOICE. INVESTORS CAN TAKE ADVANTAGE OF THIS CHOICE THROUGH A GOOD GLOBAL BALANCED FUND THAT INVESTS IN BONDS AND STOCKS OR A GLOBAL EQUITY FUND THAT INVESTS IN STOCKS ALL AROUND THE WORLD.

Investors should look outside of Canada for several reasons:

- The primary motivation for investors investing outside of Canada is higher returns. During the previous five years (ending December 1999) the best performing equity market in the world was Finland, generating an average rate of return of 56.9 per cent per year. The value of the Canadian stock market represents approximately 3 per cent of the world stock markets. Investors who ignore global investments are also ignoring 97 per cent of the investment opportunities available.

- Investors should invest outside of Canada because this will reduce the risk in a portfolio. Global stock and bond markets rise and fall at different times than do the Canadian stock and bond markets. This will ensure that investors don't place all their eggs in one basket. A poorly performing Canadian stock market could cause havoc in an investment portfolio that is highly concentrated in Canada. It is important to diversify to ensure that your investment portfolio does not get badly hit by exposure to a downturn in one region.

A global equity fund invests in stock markets around the world. These funds will have a portion of their investments invested in North America, Europe, and Asia. Some of these funds will own hundreds of securities in order to participate in the growth prospects of many firms while diversifying the risk associated with investing in different companies. A good global equity fund will be a foundation for a well-diversified mutual fund portfolio for almost any investor. Investors could consider including the AGF International Value Fund, the BPI Global Equity Fund, or the Fidelity International Portfolio Fund in their portfolios.

A global balanced fund is a fund that invests in both stock and bond markets around the world. These funds will also always have a portion of their investments invested in stock and bond markets located in North America, Europe, and Asia. They are more conservative than global equity funds because they invest in a combination of stocks and bonds, which will affect the fund's performance. Over the long term these funds will provide a lower rate of return for investors but they will also exhibit a lot less risk than a global equity fund. They exhibit less risk because bonds are less volatile than stocks; they do not decline in value to the same magnitude or at the same time as global equity funds. A conservative investor should find a good global balanced fund that will serve as a good foundation for a diversified portfolio.

Mutual Funds on Sale—Get Them Here!

Tip 38

YOU CAN BUY THE INVESTMENTS OF A MUTUAL FUND AT SALE PRICES BY LOOK-
ING AT THE SHARES OF CLOSED END FUNDS. A CLOSED-END FUND IS AN
INVESTMENT COMPANY THAT ISSUES A FIXED NUMBER OF UNITS OR SHARES AT
A SPECIFIC DATE. THE SHARES OF THIS COMPANY, THE CLOSED-END MUTUAL
FUND, ARE TRADED ON A STOCK EXCHANGE. JUST LIKE OTHER PUBLICLY
TRADED SECURITIES, THE PRICE OF A CLOSED-END FUND FLUCTUATES ACCORD-
ING TO SUPPLY AND DEMAND.

The major distinction between closed-end funds and the more traditional open-end funds
is how investors buy units. All open-end funds offer new shares on a continuous basis at a
price equal to the Net Asset Value (NAV) of the fund. The NAV is calculated by adding all
the assets of the fund, subtracting the liabilities, and dividing by the number of shares or
units outstanding. These shares or units of an open-end fund are redeemable by the fund
on any business day at a price equal to the NAV.

The shares or units of a closed-end fund trade on the stock market. Investors can only
sell these shares when there is someone willing to buy them. The value of a share is not
determined by the NAV but by an offer made by another investor. If the offer is less than
the NAV then the fund is said to be "trading at a discount." If it is trading higher than

the NAV then the fund is "trading at a premium." Most closed-end funds do trade at a small discount.

There are some additional similarities between closed-end funds and open-end funds. First, both open-ended and closed-ended mutual funds have an investment objective and are professionally managed. The portfolio manager in both types of funds invests in accordance with the stated investment objective, which is disclosed in the prospectus. Second, there is plenty of choice with both types of funds. There are over 1000 closed-end funds on stock exchanges around the world. Some invest in bonds, some in stocks, some are highly diversified, and some focus on a specific sector.

While some closed-end funds calculate their NAV at the close of each business day, most calculate it weekly. Many publications, including *The Globe & Mail, The National Post,* and *The Wall Street Journal* provide separate information on closed-end funds, including their current NAV per share, usually in the Saturday paper. Investors must consider if a closed-end fund will help them meet their long-term financial objectives, but they do offer some unique features that an open-end mutual fund doesn't. Specifically, closed-end funds offer more opportunities to customize a portfolio by focusing their investment on a single country or sector. In addition, some closed-end funds will use leverage in their investments, or place their money in a combination of unique investments. These features can enhance the risk and return characteristics of your portfolio.

Six

Investing in Specialty Funds

The primary focus of this section will be specialty funds, and with over 26 different investment categories ranging from money market to international small cap, investors have a lot of choice. However, investors have not fully utilized the benefits of specialty funds. These funds are unique because they offer investors the potential for higher rates of return while reducing the risk of the overall mutual fund portfolio over the long term. It is extremely important to remember that some specialty funds exhibit a lot of risk in isolation but when you invest a portion of your portfolio in a combination of specialty funds you can increase your returns without increasing your risk.

The table below itemizes the best-performing investment category each year for the previous 10 years.

YEAR	BEST INVESTMENT CATEGORY	RETURN*
1990	Foreign Bond	13.3%
1991	Financial Services	39.8%
1992	Natural Resources	28.9%
1993	Precious Metals	85.0%
1994	Japanese Equity	18.5%
1995	Health and Pharmaceutical	66.3%
1996	Financial Services	58.4%
1997	Financial Services	44.7%
1998	Telecommunications	50.4%
1999	Telecommunications	96.1%

Median Returns

You can see that each year a fund that focussed on a narrow investment category generated the highest rate of return. Thus, investors who want to achieve the highest rate of return in both the short- and long-term should consider a specialty fund within their portfolio. The following table list the specialty fund types that we feature in this book and the return potential for those funds over the long-term.

TIP NUMBER	MUTUAL FUND TYPE	RETURN POTENTIAL	INCOME POTENTIAL
Tip 39	High Yield Bonds	8%	High
Tip 40	Foreign Bonds	9%	High
Tip 41	Japanese Equity	13%	Low
Tip 42	Emerging Markets	14%	Low
Tip 43	China	15%	Low

Tip 44	Global Small Companies	15%	Low
Tip 45	Micro Cap Companies	15%	Low
Tip 46	Real Estate	10%	Moderate
Tip 47	Financial Services	12%	Moderate
Tip 48	Consumer Products	11%	Moderate
Tip 49	Demographics	13%	Low
Tip 50	Natural Resources	13%	Low
Tip 51	Telecommunications	13%	Low
Tip 52	Technology	14%	Low
Tip 53	E-Business	14%	Low
Tip 54	Health Care	14%	Low
Tip 55	Biotechnology	14%	Low
Tip 56	Labour Sponsored Venture Capital	15%	Low
	Canadian Bond Fund	8%	High
	Canadian Balanced Fund	9%	Moderate
	Canadian Equity Fund	10%	Low
	Global Equity Fund	12%	Low

Investors should remember that within a diversified portfolio of investments the risk associated with investing in a specialty fund is greatly reduced. The individual specialty fund will fluctuate in value, but the portfolio as a whole will fluctuate very little by comparison.

The table below itemizes the worst-performing investment category each year for the previous 10 years.

YEAR	WORST INVESTMENT CATEGORY	RETURN*
1990	Japanese Equity	-24.5%
1991	Precious Metals	-7.1%
1992	Japanese Equity	-9.3%
1993	Real Estate	-4.8%
1994	Asia & Pacific Rim Equity	-13.4%
1995	Latin American Equity	-16.2%
1996	Japanese Equity	-12.6%
1997	Precious Metals	-41.5%
1998	Latin American Equity	-35.4%
1999	Foreign Bond	-11.7%

Median Returns

Investors should be aware of the risk and reward characteristics of a specialty fund. The following table illustrates the risk associated with the funds that we covered in the book. You can see that most specialty funds have declined in value more than a more diversified fund, but over the long term they exhibit excellent growth potential.

TIP NUMBER	MUTUAL FUND TYPE	RISK	WORST 12-MONTH LOSS
Tip 39	High Yield Bonds	Low	-5.0%
Tip 40	Foreign Bonds	Low	-8.0%
Tip 41	Japanese Equity	High	-25.0%
Tip 42	Emerging Markets	High	-22.0%
Tip 43	China	High	-35.0%
Tip 44	Global Small Companies	High	-30.0%
Tip 45	Micro Cap Companies	High	-25.0%
Tip 46	Real Estate	Moderate	-10.0%
Tip 47	Financial Services	Moderate	-15.0%
Tip 48	Consumer Products	Moderate	-15.0%
Tip 49	Demographics	Moderate	-15.0%
Tip 50	Natural Resources	High	-25.0%
Tip 51	Telecommunications	High	-35.0%
Tip 52	Technology	High	-35.0%
Tip 53	E-Business	High	-40.0%
Tip 54	Health Care	High	-25.0%
Tip 55	Biotechnology	High	-35.0%
Tip 56	Labour Sponsored Venture Capital	High	-20.0%
	Canadian Bond Fund	Low	-7.5%
	Canadian Balanced Fund	Low	-10.0%
	Canadian Equity Fund	Moderate	-15.0%
	Global Equity Fund	Moderate	-15.0%

To reduce the risk associated with investing in specialty funds you should invest in a combination of funds. The fund that will reduce the risk the most is the fund with the least correlation to the other funds in your portfolio. The following table illustrates which fund pairs reduce each others' risk the most. You will notice that foreign bonds actually reduce risk more than any other investment category.

TIP NUMBER	MUTUAL FUND TYPE	LOW CORRELATION WITH
Tip 39	High Yield Bonds	Foreign Bonds
Tip 40	Foreign Bonds	Micro Cap Companies
Tip 41	Japanese Equity	Canadian Bond Fund
Tip 42	Emerging Markets	Canadian Bond Fund
Tip 43	China	Foreign Bonds
Tip 44	Global Small Companies	Foreign Bonds
Tip 45	Micro Cap Companies	Foreign Bonds
Tip 46	Real Estate	Foreign Bonds
Tip 47	Financial Services	Foreign Bonds
Tip 48	Consumer Products	Foreign Bonds
Tip 49	Demographics	Foreign Bonds
Tip 50	Natural Resources	Foreign Bonds
Tip 51	Telecommunications	Foreign Bonds
Tip 52	Technology	Foreign Bonds
Tip 53	E-Business	Foreign Bonds
Tip 54	Health Care	Micro Cap Companies
Tip 55	Biotechnology	Foreign Bonds
Tip 56	Labour Sponsored Venture Capital	Foreign Bonds
	Canadian Bond Fund	Labour Sponsored Venture Capital
	Canadian Balanced Fund	Foreign Bonds
	Canadian Equity Fund	Foreign Bonds
	Global Equity Fund	Foreign Bonds

The following table illustrates which investments are highly correlated. Investing in both funds in the pair won't reduce risk significantly. For example, investors won't reduce the risk associated with investing in foreign bonds significantly if they invest in Canadian bonds. The table above illustrates that foreign bonds and small caps make a better combination. Remember these tables are only an indication of one way to reduce risk, you won't eliminate risk no matter what combination of categories you use.

TIP NUMBER	MUTUAL FUND TYPE	HIGH CORRELATION WITH
Tip 39	High Yield Bonds	Canadian Bond Fund

Tip 40	Foreign Bonds	Canadian Bond Fund
Tip 41	Japanese Equity	Global Small Companies
Tip 42	Emerging Markets	Global Equity Fund
Tip 43	China	Labour Sponsored Venture Capital
Tip 44	Global Small Companies	Demographics
Tip 45	Micro Cap Companies	Canadian Equity Fund
Tip 46	Real Estate	Micro Cap Companies
Tip 47	Financial Services	Canadian Equity Fund
Tip 48	Consumer Products	Demographics
Tip 49	Demographics	Technology
Tip 50	Natural Resources	Canadian Equity Fund
Tip 51	Telecommunications	Demographics
Tip 52	Technology	Demographics
TIP 53	E-Business	Technology
Tip 54	Health Care	Biotechnology
Tip 55	Biotechnology	Health Care
Tip 56	Labour Sponsored Venture Capital	Demographics
	Canadian Bond Fund	Canadian Balanced Fund
	Canadian Balanced Fund	Canadian Equity Fund
	Canadian Equity Fund	Canadian Balanced Fund
	Global Equity Fund	Canadian Balanced Fund

The following tips discuss how investors can avoid making some common mistakes while investing in these funds, answer some common questions, and feature some specialty funds that you may want to consider in your portfolio. Conservative investors can increase their income and reduce risk by investing in high yield and foreign bonds; more aggressive investors can invest in some more aggressive countries such as Japan, China, or the emerging markets. Investors could also consider specific sectors or specialty funds. These funds focus on a specific sector of the economy, and when these sectors do well these funds will do well and outperform other investments. While they don't outperform other funds consistently, in combination they can be very effective. For example, a fund that focusses on high growth sectors such as technology or telecommunications will perform well with a fund that focusses on resources or financial services.

Higher Income from High Yield Bonds

Tip 39

TO UNDERSTAND HIGH YIELD BONDS, LET'S DEFINE WHAT A BOND IS. A BOND IS AN INTEREST-BEARING INVESTMENT THAT OBLIGES THE BORROWER TO PAY A SPECIFIC AMOUNT OF INTEREST FOR A SPECIFIC PERIOD OF TIME AND THEN AT MATURITY TO REPAY THE INVESTOR THE ORIGINAL AMOUNT OF THE LOAN. THE BEST EXAMPLE OF A BOND IS THE CANADA SAVINGS BOND (CSB). HIGH YIELD BONDS ARE BONDS ISSUED BY CORPORATIONS. THESE COMPANIES PAY INTEREST RATES HIGHER THAN THOSE OF TOP QUALITY GOVERNMENT OR CORPORATE BONDS TO ATTRACT INVESTORS. RECOGNIZED COMPANIES SUCH AS ROGERS COMMUNICATIONS ISSUE SUCH BONDS. CORPORATE ASSETS BACK THE BONDS; IN CASE OF DEFAULT, THE BONDHOLDERS HAVE A LEGAL CLAIM ON THOSE ASSETS.

High yield bonds can offer many advantages:

- As the name implies, high yield bonds frequently have higher yields. They can be called (redeemed) earlier, which is one reason investors receive higher interest payments. In general these bonds have shorter maturities. Downturns in this investment category have not been as dramatic as in other investment categories.

- High yield bonds have become a large global market and lack of liquidity is not a huge concern.

- High yield bonds are not perfectly correlated with other investment categories, especially other Canadian bonds and Canadian and global equities.

- High yield bonds have to earn higher returns in order to compensate investors for higher risk. High yield bonds tend to combine the higher returns associated with equities and the lower risk associated with bonds.

- These bonds will fluctuate based on more than just the direction of interest rates; they will also increase or decrease in value as the issuing company improves its financial performance.

During the previous five years, high yield bonds have generated superior returns compared to more conservative bond funds. However, these returns are less than those of some aggressive equity funds. Investors should invest a portion of their portfolio in this investment category to reduce their risk and increase their income and return potential. High yield bonds play an important role in a well-diversified mutual fund portfolio for both the conservative and aggressive investors.

This sector will still incur risk; but the worst downside risk displayed by this investment category was a loss of 8 per cent. Investors who want to capitalize on the opportunities of high yield bonds could consider several mutual funds including the C.I. Global High Yield Fund, the Talvest High Yield Bond Fund, and the Trimark Advantage Bond Fund.

Less Risk with Foreign Bonds

Tip 40

FOREIGN BOND FUNDS ARE IDEAL FOR INVESTORS SEEKING INCOME AND DIVERSIFICATION. FOREIGN BOND FUNDS, AS THEIR NAME SUGGESTS, INVEST IN BONDS THAT PAY THEIR INTEREST AND PRINCIPAL IN A CURRENCY OTHER THAN THE CANADIAN DOLLAR. FOREIGN GOVERNMENTS AND CORPORATIONS ISSUE THESE BONDS.

A foreign bond receives interest and generates income for investors, just like a domestic bond. It will fluctuate in value—declining when interest rates go up, and increasing when interest rates go down. Foreign bonds will also increase and decrease in value when their currency changes relative to the Canadian dollar. Investors should consider foreign bonds as an excellent investment alternative.

Why are foreign bond funds worth considering? They offer excellent diversification and return potential.

- Foreign bonds funds are poorly correlated with other investment categories, especially Canadian bonds and Canadian and global equities. Consider 1990 and 1998—both were great years for foreign bonds but bad years for both Canadian bonds and equities. Thus, foreign bonds make a great addition to a portfolio; they will reduce the risk and provide opportunities to adjust your investment mix between bonds and equities.

- Foreign bond funds are unique because they have the ability to invest throughout the world. Unlike the 1980s, Canadian interest rates are no longer among the highest interest rates in the world. To find bonds with higher returns investors should consider foreign bonds, which do offer higher returns than their domestic counterparts. For example, the European and emerging markets offer some very attractive investment alternatives.

- Changes in currency can boost returns. Since foreign bond funds invest in bonds outside of Canada, they will in turn invest in other currencies. This risk and opportunity is higher for foreign bonds because a larger portion of the bond's return is derived from changes in currency. A good foreign bond manager will add value in the fund by capitalizing on both currency and bond opportunities.

During the previous five years foreign bonds have not generated the superior returns associated with some specialty funds. However, they do add value because they can reduce portfolio risk. Thus, foreign bonds play an important role in a well-diversified mutual fund portfolio for both the conservative and aggressive investors.

This sector will incur risk—the worst downside risk displayed by this investment category was a loss of 10 per cent within a year. Investors who want to capitalize on the benefits of foreign bonds within a well-diversified investment portfolio could consider several mutual funds, including funds offered by AGF, Guardian, and Talvest.

The Comeback Kid—Japanese Equities

Tip 41

JAPAN IS EITHER HOT OR IT'S NOT. DURING THE 1990S, JAPANESE STOCK MARKETS TOOK INVESTORS FOR A ROLLER COASTER RIDE. HOWEVER, WITH VOLATILITY COMES OPPORTUNITIES, AND THERE ARE PLENTY OF PROSPECTS IN THE THIRD LARGEST ECONOMY IN THE WORLD. MUTUAL FUNDS THAT INVEST IN JAPAN HAVE NOT BEEN VERY POPULAR WITH CANADIAN INVESTORS RECENTLY. HOWEVER, INVESTORS SHOULD NOT IGNORE THE GROWTH STORY THAT IS PRESENT IN JAPAN, AS THERE ARE A LOT OF INNOVATIVE COMPANIES THERE WITH GOOD GROWTH POTENTIAL.

- Higher volatility in North American stock markets could send investors into Japan looking for less volatile growth opportunities.

- A higher Yen will attract foreign investors and should offset any setback incurred by Japanese export companies.

- There are lower interest rates in Japan and companies are trading at more reasonable valuations than the valuation displayed by the same companies a decade ago.

- For the first time in recent memory, companies are restructuring by laying off employees and divesting unprofitable assets. Companies are also merging, with banks leading this initiative. Daiichi Kangyo Bank, Industrial Bank of Japan, and Fuji Bank are in the process of forming the world's largest bank, as rated by assets.

- Deregulation is coming to Japan as the country is reducing its government sector in order to compete in a global environment.

- Innovative technology allows companies to compete through the innovation of new products. Companies such as Sony are using technology to increase productivity, reduce costs, and offer new products like the Sony Play Station 2.

- The Internet euphoria has just been introduced in Japan. The Internet is a great weapon in a company's arsenal, which can be used to improve its competitive and comparative advantage.

During the previous ten years the Japanese economy hasn't generated very good rates of return for investors. However, if 1999 (a year in which some funds were up more than 100 per cent) is an indication of things to come, it is going to be a great place to invest during the next 10 years. Growth for some companies within Japan has been exceptional

However, Japan is not out of the woods yet, as demand and growth could fall further. The Nikkei stock Index declined by more than 50 per cent in value during the 1990s. Long-term investors will be well served in a mutual fund that invests in this country although they should diversify and avoid investing more than 15 per cent of their portfolio. Investors who want to participate in the Japanese stock market could consider funds from Altamira, AGF, or Fidelity.

Emerging Markets—Not for the Faint of Heart

Tip 42

MANY OF TODAY'S TOP GLOBAL INVESTORS PUT THEIR MONEY IN REGIONS

HYPED AS "EMERGING MARKETS." JAPAN WAS CONSIDERED AN EMERGING

MARKET AS RECENTLY AS THE 1960S. THE UNITED STATES COULD HAVE BEEN

DEFINED AS AN EMERGING MARKET 100 YEARS AGO.

The World Bank defines a "developing" country as one with a per capita Gross National Product (GNP) of less than US$8626. Over 170 countries fit into this definition. While these countries have 85 per cent of the world's population, they represent only about 15 per cent of the world's stock market capitalization, or net worth. Mutual funds that focus on emerging markets tend to invest in countries such as Brazil, Mexico, Korea, Malaysia, South Africa, and Taiwan.

Why are emerging markets worth considering? These countries offer excellent growth opportunities over the longer term:

- Between 1985 and 1995 the market value of companies tracked by indices in these markets increased in value more than ten-fold. During the same period, capitalization tracked by established stock indices, such as those of Canada and the United States, increased by only three times. The higher market value can be attributed to the increase in the underlying securities—new countries were added, and new companies went public.

- Emerging markets have become a more attractive investment for investors since developing markets, through trade and investment, help create favourable economic conditions in these regions.

- The International Monetary Fund (IMF) has often intervened and provided stability when necessary.

- Some of these countries have had their markets more than double in value during a given year. During 1999 Turkey and Russia both posted gains in excess of 100 per cent.

Investors should not ignore the risk associated with investing in emerging markets. This risk can be attributed to several factors:

- Economic and political instability, and changes in government policies and leaders.

- Large currency swings, which can result in your losing money even if the local market rises.

- Limited amounts of reliable information in these regions, high transaction costs, and lack of liquidity can sometimes make it very difficult to buy or sell securities.

During the previous five years these market have been volatile. Equity-oriented investors should consider investing a portion of their portfolio in this investment category. Emerging markets will incur an above-average amount of risk—the worst downside risk displayed by this investment category was a loss of 25 to 30 per cent within a year. Investors who want to capitalize on the opportunities associated with investing in emerging markets should consider a mutual fund offered by C.I., CIBC, TD, Spectrum, or Mackenzie, many of which exhibit good potential. Each fund utilizes a different investment approach; thus investors should not expect the same return from each of the funds.

China—A Global Power

Tip 43

SOME SPECIALTY FUNDS ARE ATTRACTIVE BECAUSE THEY REDUCE THE RISK OF A PORTFOLIO, OTHERS GENERATE HIGHER LEVELS OF INCOME, AND STILL OTHERS CAN INCREASE RETURN. MUTUAL FUNDS THAT INVEST IN CHINA ARE IN A LEAGUE OF THEIR OWN—HIGH RISK COUPLED WITH THE POTENTIAL TO GENERATE HIGH RATES OF RETURN. SOME FUNDS THAT INVEST IN CHINA HAVE DECLINED BY MORE THAN 50 PER CENT IN A GIVEN YEAR WHILE IN OTHER YEARS THEY HAVE GENERATED RATES OF RETURN IN EXCESS OF 200 PER CENT. OVERALL, CHINESE AND OTHER ASIAN STOCKS ARE ATTRACTIVE BECAUSE THEY OFFER HIGHER GROWTH RATES THAN STOCKS IN MORE DEVELOPED MARKETS.

Why is China worth considering?

- Many investors believe the future will be better than the recent past. Foreign investors are again investing in the region.

- Companies are rigorously restructuring themselves to increase their competitive and comparative advantage and generate shareholder value.

- Japan has successfully implemented a "real" economic rebound that should boost good growth prospects for companies that operate in China.

- The financial sector has transformed itself; this will provide the foundation for growth.

- Labour costs are lower than in North America

- Tax rates are lower in China, and savings rates are higher.

- China is making arrangements to enter the World Trade Organization (WTO).

- Technology is still in its infancy compared to the United States. In the near term Chinese companies will be investing in technology to improve profitability.

Investors should not ignore the risks:

- a fragile economic system that could tumble

- political risk

- widely fluctuating currencies

- companies that have or will go bankrupt

During the previous five years, Chinese and Asian markets have lagged behind more developed markets. Recently these stock markets have rebounded from their lows. Over the long term, Chinese and Asian markets have outperformed Canadian stock markets, although with more risk. Only the most aggressive investors should invest a portion of their portfolio in this investment category. The risk here is very real: in just one month this category has recorded a loss of 25 to 30 per cent. These sorts of losses actually happen regularly and investors have incurred these declines as recently as 1998 and 2000. Investors who want to capitalize on the opportunities of China fund could consider the Talvest China Plus Fund. This fund posted a gain greater than 300 per cent within one year. However, investors should realize that such high returns are not generated consistently.

Investors who want to invest in Asia could also consider the Clarington Asian Fund, which invests in Japan, Taiwan, Hong Kong, Australia, and other countries in the region. Investors who want to invest in Hong Kong could consider the Fidelity Far East Fund. These funds are all closely correlated to funds that invest in China, but which also have the wider benefit of investing in countries throughout the region.

Global Small Companies—
Finding the Next Microsoft

Tip 44

A MUTUAL FUND THAT FOCUSSES ON GLOBAL SMALL COMPANIES PROVIDES
INVESTORS WITH A WHOLE NEW RANGE OF OPPORTUNITIES. SMALL CAP FUNDS
INVEST IN SMALL COMPANIES WHOSE TOTAL MARKET CAPITALIZATION RANGES
BETWEEN $50 MILLION TO $1 BILLION DOLLARS. WHILE MANY INVESTORS HAVE
INVESTED SOME PORTION OF THEIR INVESTMENTS OUTSIDE OF CANADA, FEW
HAVE FULLY UTILIZED THE BENEFITS OF INVESTING IN SMALL COMPANIES THAT
OPERATE THROUGHOUT THE GLOBE, SOME OF WHICH HAVE DISPLAYED EXCEL-
LENT RETURNS FOR THEIR INVESTORS.

The benefits of investing in global small companies include higher performance, more
diversification, and additional opportunities outside our country. Cisco Systems, Intel,
Microsoft, and Dell are several examples of companies that were once small cap stocks, but
have rapidly grown to become large cap stocks. In 1986 when Bill Gates took Microsoft
public, shares traded for US$0.39 per share (adjusted for splits). In 1999 the stock hit
US$115.

- A successful small cap stock can do wonders for your investment portfolio. Having a stock go from $5 to $100 makes even a small investment a significant investment.

- Canada has some great small cap stocks, but investing in a global small cap fund allows you to benefit from a greater variety of companies.

- Technology allows companies to compete through the innovation of new products and services and also allows small companies to grow faster than they did in the past, and faster than larger companies.

- The economic environment is favourable for small cap stocks.

- Over the long-term, small cap stocks have outperformed large cap stocks.

- Small cap stocks are currently trading at very reasonable valuations.

- Small companies are attracting capital, people, and resources to compete effectively within a global economy.

- You can achieve greater diversification by investing globally.

During the previous five years, global small companies have rewarded their investors. The funds and companies that have done well during this time frame have generally invested in the technology and telecommunications sectors. Some small companies have seen their stocks jump 10-, 20-, or 30-fold.

Equity oriented investors should consider investing a portion of their portfolio in smaller companies. This investment strategy will incur an above-average amount of risk because smaller companies are less proven than larger companies and do not have the ability to withstand economic setbacks. The worst downside risk displayed by this investment category was a loss of about 40 per cent within a year. Investors should remember that over the long-term small caps have outperformed but during the short-term they have underperformed significantly.

Investors who want to capitalize on the upside potential of small companies could consider the AGF Global Aggressive Small Companies Fund, the Signature Global Small Companies Fund, the Talvest Global Small Cap Fund, or the Templeton Global Smaller Companies Fund. Investors who want smaller companies outside of North America could consider the CIBC International Small Companies Fund.

Micro Cap Stocks—The Hidden Gems

Tip 45

IN CANADA THERE ARE ONLY FOUR MICRO-CAP MUTUAL FUNDS: THE BISSETT MICRO-CAP FUND (WHICH IS CLOSED TO NEW INVESTORS), THE SAXON STOCK FUND, THE CIBC CANADIAN EMERGING COMPANIES FUND, AND THE CLARINGTON CANADIAN MICRO-CAP FUND. ALL OF THESE FUNDS ATTEMPT TO CAPITALIZE ON OPPORTUNITIES IN SMALL AND MOSTLY IGNORED COMPANIES THAT HAVE GREAT GROWTH POTENTIAL. COMPANIES LIKE RESEARCH IN MOTION (RIM) AND SIERRA WIRELESS WERE BOTH MICRO CAP CANADIAN COMPANIES AS LITTLE AS TWO YEARS AGO BUT ARE NOW GREAT CANADIAN LARGE CAP COMPANIES.

Micro-cap companies have a market capitalization of $5 million to $75 million. Many mutual funds avoid these companies because an investment in one of these small companies won't form a meaningful part of their overall portfolio. If such a stock doubles in value, the fund may increase by only 1/2 per cent. Micro-cap funds can invest in this sector because these funds are smaller in size.

Consider some of the following compelling reasons to invest in a micro-cap fund.

- These companies are too small to be followed by most institutional investors. This makes it easier for fund managers to find undervalued companies. Once institutional investors begin to invest in these companies, stock prices usually jump.

- Micro-cap funds invest in established companies that are still small. These companies have a proven product, a competitive niche, and couple of years of history.

- Micro-cap stocks have benefitted from changing technology.

- Over the long-term, small caps have outperformed large cap stocks. From 1980 to 2000 the Nesbitt Burns Small Cap index outperformed the TSE 300 index by more than 1 per cent per year on average.

Investors who invest in this sector should be aware of some of the risks:

- Micro-cap stocks are inherently riskier than large-cap stocks because they are still in the early stages of their corporate development. The have lower sales and profits.

- There are only a small number of shares traded each day. This could make it impossible for mutual funds to sell or buy a large number of shares without affecting the price.

- Micro cap stocks do not react to general market conditions to the same extent as do large cap stocks.

- These stocks have also incurred periods of prolonged underperformance.

While there is a risk associated with investing in all equity funds, this investment category has generated good rates of return as well—sometimes appreciating in value by more than 80 per cent within a year.

Real Estate—Trust and Security

Tip 46

YOUNG PEOPLE EAGERLY ANTICIPATE THE DAY WHEN THEY CAN SAVE ENOUGH MONEY TO PURCHASE THEIR FIRST HOME, AND UNTIL THEN THEY OFTEN SAVE DILIGENTLY TO REALIZE THEIR DREAM. THE FAMILY HOME IS USUALLY THE SINGLE LARGEST INVESTMENT FOR MOST PEOPLE. THUS, ADDING TO THIS REAL ESTATE EXPOSURE BY INVESTING IN REAL ESTATE BEYOND THE HOME IS NOT ALWAYS THE MOST PRUDENT STRATEGY FROM THE POINT OF VIEW OF DIVERSIFICATION, BUT IT IS WORTH CONSIDERING BECAUSE REAL ESTATE EXHIBITS ITS OWN UNIQUE RISK AND RETURN CHARACTERISTICS.

Real estate is a unique investment category as it offers both income and growth potential for investors. During the late 1980s real estate was all the rage. Housing prices were going up, the economy was doing well, and investors poured billions into real estate. Today, real estate funds invest in Real Estate Investment Trusts and real estate companies such as Intrawest, Oxford Properties Group Inc., and Brookfield Properties Corporation. These companies are involved in the development of commercial, industrial, and residential property. The value of the real estate companies will fluctuate widely with increases and decreases in the supply and demand for the real estate. This demand is affected by factors such as population, per capita income, employment rates, vacancies, property restrictions, interest rates, and the health of the economy in general.

Why is real estate worth considering? Real estate provides income and growth.

- Lower interest rates provide a good source of financing and increase profitability and cash flow for real estate companies.

- Higher rental rates, which are happening in most major markets, will increase revenue and profits.

- Declining vacancy rates will increase company revenue.

- Very little new construction activity in the past decade has meant very little new supply, which should keep rental rates up.

- Many companies are flush with cash, and leverage tends to be far lower than in the 1980s.

- REITs have become a more popular investment alternative, with higher yields compared to fixed income investments. A well-diversified portfolio of real estate companies has the ability to generate a yield greater than 5 per cent.

During the previous ten years, real estate hasn't generated exceptional rates of return for investors. However, if 1998 and 1999 are indications of things to come, it is going to be a good place to invest during the next ten years, especially for investors who need income and stability. Growth for most companies in the real estate sector will continue through acquisition or through the development or redevelopment of their current properties. As a final caution, the industry is highly sensitive to changes in interest rates.

Long term, income-oriented investors will be well served in a mutual fund that invests in this sector, which has adequate growth potential and good income flows currently. Investors who want to participate in real estate could consider the funds offered by AGF, CIBC, Great West Life, and Mackenzie.

Financial Services—
The Billion Dollar Players

Tip 47

A MUTUAL FUND THAT FOCUSSES ON THE FINANCIAL SERVICES INDUSTRY INVESTS IN BANKS, BROKERAGE AND INVESTMENT FIRMS, MANAGEMENT OR MUTUAL FUND COMPANIES, AND INVESTMENT BANKS. HOWEVER IT CAN ALSO INCLUDE LIFE INSURANCE COMPANIES, PROPERTY AND CASUALTY INSURANCE FIRMS, CREDIT CARD ISSUERS, MORTGAGE LENDERS, AND SAVINGS AND LOAN COMPANIES.

Investors should remember that the financial services industry is very sensitive to changes in interest rates. When interest rates are expected to go up financial companies tend to decline in value. Many of these companies are heavily regulated, which limits the types of loans they can make, the interest rates they can charge, and the types of business they can enter. Thus, they may face lower growth prospects. In addition, during a recession the losses from loan defaults can negatively affect a company. But there is merit in this sector. During the previous 10 years, Canadian financial services companies generated an annualized return greater than 15 per cent. And keep in mind some other points:

- The Society for Worldwide Interbank Financial Telecommunication reported that US$2.3 trillion moves through the world's electronic network daily.

- Asset accumulation by baby boomers fueled the mutual fund industry in the 1990s. This group will continue to have an influence during the next 10 years.

- The mutual fund and insurance industry should continue to consolidate, and such takeover speculation has fueled mutual fund company stocks in the spring of 2000. Some companies stocks have appreciated in value by more than 70 per cent in three months.

- In the new millennium, Internet-generated revenues are expected to soar to more than US$1.3 trillion,[1] with financial services playing a key role.

- The increasing capital requirements of emerging economies will require financing from financial institutions.

- Global deregulation is upon us. Countries have had to reduce their infrastructure costs to compete in a global environment. This provides an opportunity for banks to consolidate.

- Technology allows companies to compete through the innovation of new products. Through the Internet you can apply for a bank loan, trade stock, and pay bills—the opportunities are infinite.

During the previous five years financial companies have rewarded their investors, and some mutual funds, investment banks, brokerage houses, and banks have had their stocks double, triple, and quadruple. Although recent performance hasn't been as impressive, the future for the industry is very encouraging. Equity-oriented investors should consider investing a portion of their portfolio in this investment category. This sector will incur an above-average amount of risk because the industry is very sensitive to interest rates. The worst downside risk displayed by this investment category was a loss of 25 to 30 per cent within a year. Investors should remember that over the long-term this sector has outperformed but during the short-term, 1999 for example, it has also underperformed significantly. Investors who want to capitalize on the opportunities of a financial services fund could consider funds offered by AIC, CIBC, C.I., and Fidelity.

[1] *Forrester Research Inc.*

Consumer Products— Investing in What You Buy

Tip 48

BY THE TIME YOU WAKE UP IN THE MORNING AND BRUSH YOUR TEETH, WASH YOUR FACE, AND SHOWER, YOU HAVE ALREADY USED THREE OR FOUR PRODUCTS THAT COMPANIES WHO OPERATE IN THE CONSUMER PRODUCTS INDUSTRY PRODUCE. A MUTUAL FUND THAT FOCUSSES ON THE CONSUMER PRODUCTS INDUSTRY INVESTS IN COMPANIES THAT MANUFACTURE AND/OR SELL THE GOODS THAT ARE USED IN DAILY LIFE: HOUSEHOLD APPLIANCES, AUTOMOBILES, CLOTHING, PERSONAL COSMETICS, ENTERTAINMENT, FOOD, HOMES, HOUSEHOLD PRODUCTS, LEISURE, PERSONAL COMPUTERS, RESORTS, RECREATION & SPORTS, RESTAURANTS, AND TRAVEL AND ACCOMMODATION. MANY OF THE MUTUAL FUNDS IN THIS SECTOR INVEST PRIMARILY IN THE UNITED STATES BUT WILL INVEST A SMALL PORTION IN OTHER COUNTRIES.

Investors should note that this industry is very sensitive to changes in consumer spending. When consumers have money to spend and are optimistic about the future, demand for consumer goods increases. This scenario was obvious during Christmas 1999 as consumer optimism produced record sales in many retail stores. However, during a recession consumer product companies usually see sales and profits either remain stable or decline, and stock prices remain stable or decline.

Why are consumer products worth considering? This sector has penetrated every part of our personal and professional lives. That is the beauty of this industry—clients have to come back for more products and services again and again. You can make do with your old car for another year, but you can't do without new soap, shampoo, and shaving products. Consider the following trends:

- Consumers tend to spend more than they earn, fuelling growth in the overall economy and especially in the consumer products industry.

- World per person income is increasing according to Standard & Poor's DRI (an economic forecasting and consulting company). This trend is especially apparent in developing countries. Thus, the number of people that can afford consumer products is increasing.

- Lower taxes, a general trend throughout the world, means more money in the pocket of the consumer.

- Changes in technology have allowed companies to provide products and services at a lower price, thereby increasing demand and profits.

Equity-oriented investors should consider investing a portion of their portfolio in the consumer products sector. This sector will incur an above-average amount of risk because the industry is very sensitive to consumer spending. The worst downside risk displayed by this investment category was a loss of 25 to 30 per cent within a year. Investors who want to capitalize on the opportunities in the consumer products sector could consider the C.I. Consumer Products Fund or the Fidelity Focus Consumer Industries Fund.

Demographics—
Profiting from Baby Boomers

Tip 49

BABY BOOMERS, THOSE BORN IN THE POST-WAR ERA BETWEEN 1945 AND 1955,

ARE THE SINGLE LARGEST SEGMENT OF THE NORTH AMERICAN POPULATION.

SINCE THEY REPRESENT SUCH A LARGE SEGMENT OF THE POPULATION, MANY

COMPANIES FREQUENTLY TARGET BABY BOOMERS FOR THEIR PRODUCTS AND

SERVICES. BEING ABLE TO CORRECTLY PREDICT WHAT PRODUCTS AND SERVICES

THIS GROUP IS GOING TO ACQUIRE IN THE NEXT PHASE OF THEIR LIFE HAS MADE

SOME COMPANIES VERY PROFITABLE AND THEIR SHAREHOLDERS VERY RICH.

During the 1980s baby boomers were frequently credited with driving real estate markets to record highs. Once baby boomers completed their home buying, demand declined and real estate prices soured. In the early 1990s, faced with low GIC rates, baby boomers poured billions of dollars into mutual funds and some mutual fund companies had the value of their stocks double or triple within a year. Companies that have the ability to capitalize on this demographic segment have the ability to generate high rates of return for their investors. Higher returns are made possible because baby boomers are such a large segment of the population. Providing a product or service that baby boomers want should insure a company's success with above-average growth.

Consider the changing demographics of the Canadian population. Many are a direct result of baby boomers getting older. Successful companies will have to target an older, wiser, and wealthier consumer. Consider the following:

- The number of Canadians age 75+ will grow by 78 per cent by 2011.

- The number of Canadians age 65–74 will grow by 135 per cent by 2011.

- The "over 85" age group is the fastest growing age bracket in Canada. It will triple by 2011.

- Canadians are having fewer children.

- 18% of people over age 65 have no living children.

- The average married couple will have more living parents than living children by the year 2020.

There are several mutual funds whose investment objective is to place their money in companies that provide products and services to baby boomers. These funds usually invest in the leisure, recreation, technology, telecommunications, financial, consumer products, and industrial products sectors of the economy. These sectors are well positioned to meet the demands of an older consumer.

During the previous five years growth in this industry has been good. However, investors active in this segment of the market are still incurring risk, as some of these investments have declined in value by more than 30 per cent within a year. Investors should diversify in a portfolio of mutual funds and avoid investing more than 10 per cent of their portfolio in the sector. Investors who want to capitalize on this demographic trend could consider several mutual funds offered by AIC, C.I., or CIBC.

Resources—The Overlooked Treasure

Tip 50

COMPARED TO OTHER DEVELOPED COUNTRIES, THE RESOURCE SECTOR HAS ALWAYS MADE UP A HUGE CHUNK OF CANADA'S ECONOMY. CANADA HAS A WEALTH OF NATURAL RESOURCES AND COMPANIES IN THIS COUNTRY HAVE THE ABILITY TO EXTRACT AND COMMERCIALIZE THOSE RESOURCES EFFECTIVELY AND EFFICIENTLY. HISTORICALLY, RESOURCE INVESTMENTS HAVE ALWAYS BEEN VERY VOLATILE BUT INVESTORS SHOULD REALIZE THAT VOLATILITY CREATES INVESTMENT OPPORTUNITIES. RESOURCE STOCKS HAVE GENERATED RETURNS GREATER THAN 100 PER CENT WITHIN ONE YEAR, ALTHOUGH INVESTORS SHOULD BE AWARE THAT THIS SECTOR HAS ALSO EXHIBITED DOWNSIDE VOLATILITY.

The resource sector includes agriculture, energy, metals, minerals, natural gas, oil, paper and forest products, and gold and other precious metals. This sector is volatile because of the cyclical nature of the industry: it increases and decreases in value with the rise and fall in value of the underlying commodity prices. Oil, copper, and gold are examples of base commodities; and higher commodity prices mean more profit for the companies that pull the oil, copper, and gold out of the ground.

Prudent investors who buy low (when the underlying commodity prices are low) and sell high (when those commodity prices are high) have the potential to earn a good return on their investments in the resource sector. Overall growth is also fuelled by decreases in proven supplies of the commodity, as well as by increases in consumer and industrial demand. For example, the demand for oil in North America continues to grow, and the U.S. Department of Energy has estimated that by 2015 oil consumption will be 50 per cent higher than in 1995.

Resource stocks could be a good investment for investors because they are currently exhibiting real value—their stock price is very low compared to the underlying assets. Consider some of the favourable factors influencing the resource sector.

- When there are clear signs of a good and sustainable economic recovery, like the economic recovery in Japan that is taking shape currently, resource stocks begin to outperform. The recovery in Japan is associated with good economic strength in Asia, Europe, and North America.

- Output levels of oil and other commodities have been restricted, thus reducing supply and increasing commodity prices.

- Resource companies are earning bigger profits and producing excellent cash flow growth.

- Most resource stocks are conservatively valued; some stocks are selling at their lowest valuations in history.

- Resource companies can be a hedge against inflation.

During the previous five years growth in this industry has been very weak and most resource funds have had a very rough ride. However, there are opportunities, as some companies within the industry are cash rich; they have good reserves and have added value for their shareholders. Investors who want to participate in this sector could consider the C.I. Global Resource Fund, or the Trimark Canadian Resource Fund for a well-diversified fund.

Telecommunications—At Our Fingertips

Tip 51

WHEN ALEXANDER GRAHAM BELL FIRST INVENTED THE TELEPHONE IN 1876, NO ONE KNEW IT WOULD BECOME SUCH A VITAL COMPONENT OF OUR LIVES. WE HAVE SEEN ADVANCES IN THIS TECHNOLOGY SO THAT WE CAN SHOP, TALK, BANK, AND WORK IN A GLOBAL MARKETPLACE. FROM SPEAKING TO A FRIEND NEXT DOOR OR OVERSEAS, TO SENDING OR RECEIVING E-MAIL OVER TELEPHONE LINES, WE ALL RELY ON THE TELECOMMUNICATIONS INDUSTRY. MOVING AWAY FROM THE TRADITIONAL TELEPHONE, THE INTERNET, MEDIA, TELEVISION, AND SATELLITES ARE EXAMPLES OF HOW THE TELECOMMUNICATIONS INDUSTRY HAS BROADENED. IN THE NEXT MILLENNIUM THE TELECOMMUNICATIONS INDUSTRY WILL BE A KEY AREA OF THE GLOBAL ECONOMY, AND SHOULD CONTINUE TO GROW AS CORPORATIONS CHANGE FROM OLDER ANALOG COPPER WIRING TO DIGITAL FIBER OPTIC LINES TO INCREASE SPEED AND ENHANCE SERVICE FOR THEIR CLIENTS.

The growth potential is the key to this sector.

- There is explosive growth in telecommunications services in developing nations.

- Demand for phone service, cellular phone service, and the Internet is higher than the near-term supply

- In the United States the telecom industry is estimated to be worth $2 trillion.[1]

- Telephone lines have increased tenfold during the previous 40 years.

- In the previous four years the number of Internet users went from 3 million to 100 million.

Why is the industry growing so fast? There are five reasons:

1 Globalization. Larger companies have the ability to identify and capitalize on new growth opportunities.

2 Deregulation. In 1997, 69 countries signed the World Trade Organization agreement to deregulate many of their industries. This provided the catalyst to allow companies to compete in various markets around the world that were traditionally protected from foreign competition.

3 Technology. This allows companies to compete through the innovation of new products.

4 The Internet. The Net has generated new demand for telecommunications in the new economy. Phone companies now have to direct both voice and data traffic.

5 New demand. Internet users, developing markets, and current users are all demanding more and more from their telecommunications provider.

During the previous five years growth in this industry has been exceptional. However, investors should realize that this sector could still incur some downside risk, as demand could decline and many of these companies are currently highly valued. Small changes in the underlying fundamentals could trigger a large sell-off in the short-term. However, long-term investors will be well served in a mutual fund that invests in this sector, although they should avoid investing more than 10 per cent of their portfolio in this area. Investors who want to participate in this sector could consider a fund from AIM, C.I., Fidelity, or Spectrum. These funds have appreciated by more than 100 per cent within a year. These high rates of return can significantly increase the size of an investor's portfolio, but come with associated volatility and downside risk.

[1] *International Telecommunications Union*

Technology—Changing the World

Tip 52

GLOBAL TECHNOLOGY SPENDING HAS ACCELERATED TO US$3 TRILLION IN THE 1990S, FOUR TIMES HIGHER THAN TECHNOLOGY SPENDING IN THE 1980S.[1] THIS SECTOR INCLUDES SUCH INDUSTRIES AS COMPUTER SERVICES, SOFTWARE, AND SYSTEMS; COMMUNICATIONS SYSTEMS; ELECTRONICS; OFFICE EQUIPMENT; SCIENTIFIC INSTRUMENTS; AND SEMICONDUCTORS.

Growth is the one word behind all of the interest in this sector.

- There is explosive growth in telecommunications needs in developing nations.
- Demand for the Internet is higher than the supply. In this millennium, Internet-generated revenues are expected to soar to more than US$1.3 trillion.[2]
- Personal computer demand is expected to grow exponentially worldwide. Computer expenditures as a percentage of Gross Domestic Product (GDP) will increase to 8.5 per cent.[3]
- In this new millennium, wireless communications spending could reach $80 billion.[4]
- In the previous four years the number of Internet users went from 3 million to 100 million.

Why is the industry growing so fast and why is it so important? Four reasons:

1. Globalization. Larger "new economy" companies have the ability to identify and capitalize on new growth opportunities, not just domestically but globally.

2. Deregulation. Countries have been selling off their infrastructure in order to compete in a global environment.

3. Technology. This allows companies to compete through the innovation of new products. Companies can increase productivity and reduce costs, and offer new products and services that increase sales.

4. The Internet. Using the Internet introduces a new weapon that can improve a company's competitive and comparative advantage.

If you still have doubts about the role of technology in the new millennium consider what Jack Welsh, CEO of General Electric, recently stated, "This company's number 1, number 2, number 3, and number 4 priorities are e-commerce."

During the previous five years growth in this industry has been exceptional. Some companies, such as America Online (AOL) have come from nowhere and built sustainable franchises within a few years. However, this sector will still exhibit downside risk (remember April 2000 when the NASDAQ declined by 25.8 per cent in just one week?). However, long-term investors will be well served in a mutual fund that invests in this high growth, high risk sector although they should avoid investing more than 10 per cent of their portfolio in this area.

Some of the following mutual funds have appreciated in value by more than 250 per cent within one year, and while investors should not expect the same return every year, it is reasonable to look for some above-average rates of return. Investors who want to participate in this sector could consider the AIM Global Technology Fund, Altamira Science & Technology Fund, and Talvest Global Science and Technology Fund. Investors saving for retirement could also consider the RRSP-eligible clone funds offered by these companies.

[1] *The New Economy, Dr Ed Yardeni, www.yardeni.com*

[2] *Forrester Research Inc.*

[3] *The New Economy, Dr Ed Yardeni*

[4] *MultiMedia Telecommunications Association*

Invest in e-business—The Next Revolution

Tip 53

TWO THINGS ARE CLEAR IN BUSINESS; THE INTERNET HAS GENERATED SWEEP-ING CHANGES IN THE WAY BUSINESS COMPETES, AND NET-BASED BUSINESS SOLUTIONS ARE HERE TO STAY. THIS COMPONENT OF THE BUSINESS WORLD HAS BECOME ENORMOUS AND INVESTORS JUST CAN'T AFFORD TO IGNORE IT FOR THE LONG TERM. YES, THERE WILL BE VOLATILITY—THE MARKETS' BEHAV-IOUR IN APRIL AND MAY 2000 COME TO MIND—BUT IN THE FALL OF 1999 THERE WAS TREMENDOUS GROWTH, WHICH GENERATED MANY TRIPLE-DIGIT RETURNS FOR ASTUTE INVESTORS. MANY INVESTORS HAVE ALREADY INVESTED BILLIONS OF DOLLARS INTO TECHNOLOGY IN GENERAL, BUT INVESTORS COULD ALSO CONSIDER A FUND THAT FOCUSSES ON BUSINESS-TO-BUSINESS ELECTRONIC APPLICATIONS, CALLED E-BUSINESS OR E-COMMERCE, WHICH FALL INTO MORE NARROWLY DEFINED SEGMENTS OF THE TECHNOLOGY INDUSTRY.

Investors could consider this segment because there is great growth potential for companies that focus on the business-to-business market. Currently consumers generate the largest portion of online sales but Goldman Sachs, a leading U.S. brokerage firm, expects business-to-business sales to rise to US$1.5 trillion by the year 2004 from US$39 billion in 1998.

Why is business-to-business hot?

- Companies want to save money by using the Internet. Companies can conduct almost all of their business on the Internet, from purchasing raw materials to servicing their customers. The end result is a cost reduction ranging from 5 to 30 per cent. These savings are a direct result of better logistics that result in better prices for raw materials, less waste, and less inventory.

- Companies want to increase revenue, and the Internet provides new opportunities to source and attract new customers.

- Major corporations are stating that the Internet is the way they want to interact with suppliers in the near future.

As the previous tip described, growth in the technology industry has been exceptional and according to some, the growth has only begun in the business-to-business segment of the market. Some companies, such as JDS Uniphase, have come from nowhere and built sustainable franchises within a few years. However, this sector will still exhibit downside risk (for example, during April 2000, the NASDAQ declined by 25.8 per cent in just one week). Demand and overall sector growth could decline, and many of these companies are richly valued at present despite recent market setbacks. Aggressive investors who are well diversified should consider investing a portion of their money is this sector.

Some of the following mutual funds have appreciated in value by more than 250 per cent within one year, and while investors should not expect the same return every year, it is reasonable to look for some above-average rates of return. Investors who want to participate in this narrow sector with high risks and high growth potential could consider the Altamira e-business Fund, the C.I. Global Business-to-Business Fund, or the Royal e-commerce Fund. All of these funds will have an emphasis on e-business companies.

Health Care—A New Millennium

Tip 54

THE HEALTH CARE SECTOR MAKES PEOPLE BETTER, AND CAN MAKE YOUR WALLET BETTER AS WELL. THIS SECTOR PRODUCES THE REQUIRED GOODS AND SERVICES THAT ALLOW HEALTH CARE PROFESSIONALS TO TREAT AND PREVENT SICKNESS. THE HEALTH CARE INDUSTRY INCLUDES BIOTECHNOLOGY FIRMS, HEALTH MAINTENANCE ORGANIZATIONS, MEDICAL DEVICES, AND COMPANIES THAT OPERATE IN HOSPITAL MANAGEMENT, PHARMACEUTICALS, AND MEDICAL PRODUCTION.

Growth in this sector is fueled by favourable demographic trends that are both global and lasting. An aging population, higher demand for health services, and increased pressure to reduce costs will provide opportunities for some companies and their astute investors. Morgan Stanley, a leading U.S. brokerage firm, has estimated that the global capitalization for health sciences to be US$1 trillion in 2000.

The health field is hot for the following reasons:

- The life expectancy in developed countries is 78 years, which is significantly higher than the life expectancy in the least developed countries, which is 43 years.[1] Higher life expectancy means higher demand for the products and services that increase life expectancy. People over the age of 65 spend 10 times more on health care than any other group does.

- The World Health Organization expects the population aged 65 and over in developed countries to increase by 200 to 400 per cent in the next 30 years.

- As the baby boomers age, they will spend more on health care than ever before.

- Health care companies spend big money on research and development, which will further advance the industry as they introduce new products and services.

During the previous five years, growth in this industry has been exceptional. Although the sector has incurred some short-term setbacks, the long-term fundamentals remain intact. Some companies like Warner Lambert, Merck & Co, and Johnson & Johnson have built sustainable franchises while creating value for their shareholders. However, this sector will still incur downside risk. In just one month, March 2000, most of these funds declined in value by at least 20 per cent. Many of these companies need to continue to develop and refine new products to keep earnings up. These same companies are also highly regulated, and the process to receive government approval of new products could affect the share price of these companies. In addition, products could become obsolete due to changes in technology.

However, long-term investors will be well served in a mutual fund that invests in this high growth, high risk sector, although they should avoid investing more than 5 to 10 per cent of their portfolio in the sector. Some of these funds have generated returns greater than 100 per cent within a year but investors shouldn't expect these returns every year. Investors who want to participate in this sector could consider the AIM Global Health Sciences Fund, the C.I. Global Health Sciences Fund, the Fidelity Focus Health Care Fund, and the Talvest Global Health Care Fund. Investors saving for retirement could also consider the RRSP eligible clone funds offered by these companies.

[1] *World Health Organization*

Biotechnology—
Dynamic and Leading Edge

Tip 55

THE CONCEPT BEHIND BIOTECHNOLOGY IS SIMPLE —MAKE PRODUCTS THAT MAKE PEOPLE HEALTHY AND YOU CAN MAKE LARGE PROFITS FOR SHAREHOLDERS. BIOTECHNOLOGY IS ONE OF THE MOST EXCITING AND DYNAMIC FIELDS OF HEALTH CARE TODAY. IT PURSUES THE ADVANCEMENT OF LEADING-EDGE MEDICAL BREAKTHROUGHS. RECENTLY INVESTORS HAVE STARTED A MARKET "BUZZ" AROUND THE POTENTIAL FOR BIOTECHNOLOGY COMPANIES THAT CAN ANALYZE AND MANIPULATE GENETIC INFORMATION TO DEVELOP NEW DRUGS AND TREATMENTS.

Growth in this sector is fueled by favourable demographic trends, which are global in nature and will persist into the future. With higher research and development budgets and changes in technology, the industry will likely generate some exceptional new products in the near future.

Why is biotechnology hot? In addition to the reasons that the health care industry as a whole is booming, biotechnology companies have some additional advantages:

- According to the U.K. company Nycomed Amersham there are now over 350 different biotechnology drugs in the pipeline, up from 75 in 1989.

- Mergers and acquisitions will take place as large pharmaceutical firms buy small biotechnology firms for their innovative and effective products. Small firms hope to be acquired because they do not have the resources to establish their own distribution channels.

During the previous five years, growth in this industry has been good. Although the sector has incurred some short-term setbacks (in March 2000 this sector declined in value by more than 20 per cent) the long-term fundamentals remain intact. Some companies like Chiron Corporation, Genentech Corporation, and Andrx Corporation have all begun the development of new drugs. However, investors should remember that this sector does display downside risk, and they should be prepared for short-term volatility. Demand for various drugs could also decline, which would affect growth. In addition, many of these small companies need to continue to develop products while maintaining a prudent capital structure and avoiding bankruptcy. Most of these companies are highly regulated, and the process to receive government approval from the Food and Drug Association (FDA) in the United States could affect the share price of these companies. In addition, products could become obsolete due to changes in technology.

However, long-term investors will be well served in a mutual fund that invests in this high growth, high risk sector, although they should avoid investing more than 5 per cent of their portfolio in this one area. Investors who want to participate in this sector could consider the C.I. Global Biotechnology Fund. Investors who want to consider a more diversified health care fund could consider the AIM Global Health Sciences Fund, the Fidelity Focus Health Care Fund, or the Talvest Global Health Care Fund. Investors saving for retirement could also consider the RRSP-eligible clone funds offered by these companies. Some of these funds have generated a return greater than 50 per cent within six months.

Getting Free Money
with Labour Sponsored Funds

Tip 56

A LABOUR-SPONSORED VENTURE CAPITAL CORPORATION (LSVCC), SO CALLED BECAUSE A UNION GROUP HAS TO SPONSOR THE FUND, IS A MUTUAL FUND THAT INVESTS IN HIGH GROWTH AND HIGH-RISK EARLY STAGE COMPANIES BEFORE THEY BECOME PUBLICLY TRADED. THE ATTRACTION HERE IS THE POTENTIAL FOR HIGHER RATES OF RETURN. MORGAN STANLEY REPORTED THAT THE AVERAGE ANNUAL RATE OF RETURN ON VENTURE CAPITAL DURING THE PREVIOUS 20 YEARS WAS 21.4 PER CENT, WHICH WAS 3.9 PER CENT HIGHER THAN FOR SMALL CAP STOCKS.

The opportunities for investors are great:

- Venture capital firms invest in early and late stage entrepreneurial companies before they become publicly traded companies. This allows them to invest in the company before other investors and thus they have the ability to participate in higher rates of return.

- Venture capital funds are not susceptible to the short-term volatility of the stock market. Most of the companies a venture capital firm owns are not traded on the stock exchange and thus do not encounter the daily gyrations of the market. However, reduced overall portfolio volatility does not mean that there is little risk with these funds. The risk, as well as the opportunity, can be very large.

- The government offers financial incentives. Individuals who invest in a labour-sponsored fund will receive a 15 per cent tax credit from the federal government, up to $750 annually. In addition, investors could receive an additional 15 per cent tax credit from their provincial government, depending on their province of residence. In return, investors have to invest in the fund for eight years. If they redeem the fund before this time, they will have to repay the tax credit.

- When you invest in these funds within a self-directed RRSP, for each $1 you invest in such a fund you will be able to increase your foreign investments by $3 to maximum of 45 per cent (50 per cent in 2001). Thus, if you have $50 000 in your RRSP and you have $12 500 invested outside of Canada, with an additional $5000 in a labour-sponsored fund into your RRSP, you can invest an additional $15 000 in foreign investments.

The past five years have not generated eye-popping results for most of these funds. However, recently some of these funds have been able to exploit several successful investments, and some funds have doubled in value within a very short time frame. Long-term investors will be well served in a mutual fund that invests in this high growth, high-risk venture capital market. The key to selecting a good labour-sponsored mutual fund is the quality of the fund's management. Management must have the ability to find and invest in good quality start-up business that has above-average growth prospects at a reasonable price. Investors who want to participate in this sector could consider any of 17 different mutual funds (some of which are not available in every province) including the B.E.S.T. Discoveries Fund, Centerfire Growth Fund, the Canadian Science & Technology Fund, the Triax Growth Fund, or the Vengrowth Fund.

Seven

More Investment Options

When you shop for everything from food to cars, you realize that there is a great deal of choice in the marketplace—from products to places to make your purchases. In the investment industry there is a similar range of options. You can choose from different bonds and Guaranteed Income Certificates (GICs), you can pick from thousands of different mutual funds from hundreds of different mutual fund providers, and if that's not enough you can choose from an even larger number of stocks. The objective of this chapter is to help you make heads and tails out of most of these choices. To keep each tip to a manageable size we have limited our coverage to the most important factors present in each of these investment options, which will serve to start your investment research.

Most refreshingly, this chapter allows investors to explore investment alternatives outside of traditional mutual funds and bank deposits. Many, but not all of these investments are higher risk—a notable exception are Canada Savings Bonds (CSBs), which are very conservative and allow investors to earn income while keeping their investment secure. We also introduce you to some of the most common GICs. There have been a lot of changes in this area during the previous three years, with the result being that investors should be pleasantly surprised by all of the choices that they have. We also visit the often-overlooked investment of bonds, and how they can help you secure the income you want. Many investors feel that bonds are boring and mostly the same, but we will introduce you to convertible bonds, which are bonds with all the income potential of traditional bonds but also have the upside potential associated with common stocks. In addition, we will introduce strip bonds, which pay no interest until the bond matures.

Next we dive into alternative growth investments with names such as iUnits, SPDRS, DIAMONDS, and WEBS. All these investments are index-based funds that trade on stock exchanges. We will also introduce common stock investments and highlight the benefits of owning stocks directly in your investment account. For investors who have maximized their RRSP we will introduce you to a life insurance policy that will help you save tax when making investments.

In concluding the chapter we will introduce pooled funds, which are much like mutual funds but with lower management fees, but which have higher minimum investments. More aggressive, income-oriented investors could consider investing in royalty investment trusts or real estate investment trusts, both of which have their advantages and risks. Or, how about participating in an Initial Public Offering (IPO), investing in options, hedge funds, or futures? Just check out the last four tips of this chapter to get you started.

Investors who put their money in some of these investments will soon realize that each alternative has its own unique return and risk characteristics. Investors should diversify their portfolio while investing in some traditional and non-traditional investments. Over the long-term this will allow you to earn a higher rate of return without increasing your risk.

Canada Savings Bonds—
How They Can Work for You

Tip 57

THE FINANCIAL SERVICES INDUSTRY HAS DEVELOPED NEW AND INNOVATIVE PRODUCTS DURING THE PAST DECADE. SOME OF THE CHANGES IN THE INVESTMENT WORLD ARE EVEN CATCHING UP TO ONE OF THE ELDER STATESMEN OF INVESTMENTS: THE CANADA SAVINGS BOND (CSB). THE CANADIAN GOVERNMENT ISSUES CSBS IN ORDER TO FINANCE THE GOVERNMENT'S EXPENDITURES. SOME RECENT CHANGES HAVE MADE THESE SAVINGS CERTIFICATES MORE APPEALING FOR THE "CASH" COMPONENT OF AN INVESTMENT PORTFOLIO. INVESTORS WHO WANT TO RECEIVE COMPETITIVE INTEREST RATES WILL FIND CSBS AN IDEAL, LOW RISK, AND STABLE INVESTMENT.

The basics haven't changed much. Canada Savings Bonds may be bought almost anywhere, from banks and credit unions to full service and discount brokerages (although they might not be heavily advertised at the latter outlets). They are available for only a set period every year, generally from the fall to the spring, and may be cashed in at any time, although if they are redeemed within three months of purchase no interest is paid. Minimum rates of interest are set, and may be raised if market conditions change.

Compound Interest Savings Bonds, where interest payable is reinvested, are now available to be held directly in an RRSP. In other words, while it is possible to hold these bonds within a self-directed RRSP, they can also be held directly in a Registered Plan, with no extra fees or restrictions other than a minimum purchase of $500. These bonds can also be held in a RRIF, again with a no fee option. Regular Interest Bonds are also available, where interest is paid annually, but they cannot be held within an RRSP or a RRIF.

A newer form of investment is called the Canada Premium Bond (CPB). They are very similar to traditional CSBs and can be purchased between the fall and the spring. These bonds are available wherever Canada Savings Bonds are sold. They pay a moderately higher interest rate, in exchange for which they are only redeemable on the anniversary of the issue date. They too can be held directly in an RRSP, and are also subject to a minimum $500 purchase. Since their introduction, they have proven to be popular, and sales now match those of traditional Canada Savings Bonds. Both Premium Bonds and Savings Bonds are fully guaranteed by the Government of Canada, making them the ideal risk-free investment.

While today's low interest rates and rising equity prices may seem to make CSBs an antiquated idea, they do have some advantages when compared to GICs or money market accounts. Canada Savings Bonds may be purchased for as little as $100, far below the minimum requirements of other investments. Compound Interest Bonds are also available through payroll deduction plans, which are available through many employers. Such forced savings plans, where money is immediately deducted from a paycheque and used to purchase CSBs, is a widely appealing and easily implemented concept that will allow you to increase your investments over time.

More information can be found at www.cis-pec.gc.ca, or at www.csb.gc.ca, or by calling 1-800-575-5151.

The Changing GIC Arena

Tip 58

EVER WATCH LAWN BOWLING ON A BLACK AND WHITE TV? FOR THE LONGEST TIME THE GUARANTEED INVESTMENT CERTIFICATE (GIC) WORLD WAS AS STAID AND PLACID AS THIS. DURING THE 1980S, THE MAJOR AREA FOR FLEXIBILITY CAME FROM CHOOSING THE FINANCIAL INSTITUTION THAT OFFERED THE HIGHEST RATE. IN THE 1990S, INTEREST RATES DROPPED AND A SOARING EQUITY MARKET FUELLED INVESTORS' INTEREST IN MUTUAL FUNDS. IN TURN, FINANCIAL INSTITUTIONS INTRODUCED NEW FORMS OF GICS, WHICH RESULTED IN A MARKETPLACE WITH MORE CHOICE FOR INVESTORS.

While each bank or savings institution adds their own bells or whistles to a traditional GIC, there are a few broad categories for these investments:

- Cashable or Redeemable GICs. As their name suggests, and unlike traditional GICs, these products offer the flexibility of cashing out all or just some of your investment after a certain length of time (often 90 days just like Canada Savings Bonds). In return they typically offer a lower rate of return than traditional GICs but are very competitive to other short-term investments.

- Escalating Rate GICs. These products offer a set rate for only the first year or two. After that the rate changes over the fixed term of the GIC. While there is some flexibility here, what matters most is the rate of interest you will receive over the whole term of the investment, and this is often not much more than a regular GIC.

- Laddered GICs. These are like a traditional GIC, but your investment is split over the (typically) five-year term. What this means is that a fifth of your money, in this example, comes due every year. While this is fine in periods of low and rising interest rates, you can miss out on "locking in" higher rates for the long-term.

- Linked GICs. The interest rates for linked GICs float up and down, and are tied to some benchmark rate. Often there is a minimum floor beneath which rates are guaranteed not to fall, in a method very much like Canada Savings Bonds.

- Stock Market Linked GICs. These are one of the hottest sellers of late, and offer protection of capital (upon maturity your initial investment is returned) combined with some participation in the appreciation of a stock market index. While this may seem like the best of all possible worlds, there are some caveats. First, while your capital is protected, most of these products offer little or no guaranteed minimum rate of return. If stocks don't rise, or if they fall, you would have done better in any of the other types of GICs. Secondly, many sellers limit or cap the potential returns from the market index, so that often growth is limited to only 50% of the appreciation of the overall stock market. As well, investors lose out on the dividends that the stocks in the index would otherwise be paying during the course of the investment.

Don't Forget About Bonds

Tip 59

IN HOCKEY OR SOCCER, THE LAST DEFENCE IS THE GOALIE. IN INVESTING A GOOD BOND SERVES THE SAME FUNCTION, DEFENDING YOUR PORTFOLIO FROM SEVERE DOWNTURNS. FOR MOST OF THE PAST DECADE THE STRONG EQUITY MARKET HAS EASILY OVERSHADOWED THE MORE MODEST BOND MARKET, YET FIXED INCOME INVESTMENTS, INCLUDING BONDS, MERIT SOME PLACE IN NEARLY EVERY INVESTOR'S PORTFOLIO.

You should consider investing in bonds for both income and stability. In any given year equity markets could appreciate in value by 30 to 40 per cent or decline in value by the same amount. Bonds fluctuate far less. Bonds also pay interest on a regular basis and thus investors will receive a cheque each month or quarter.

As with any investment, it is easy to get lost in the minutiae and with bonds the details come from some of the arithmetical calculations that determine the yields, returns, and risk of a bond. Here are the basics. Bonds offer a fixed amount of interest (the coupon rate), until a fixed period of time (the maturity date) at which point the denomination, also called the face value, is repaid and the interest payments stop. Bonds are issued by the federal, provincial, and municipal governments, and by a wide variety of corporations.

In general, corporations have to offer higher coupon rates to sell their bonds than the lower rates attached to the relative safety of provincial and Government of Canada bonds. Maturity dates range from 1 year to more than 30 years, with higher coupon rates being associated with longer periods to maturity, to compensate for increased risk. Long-term bonds tend to rise and fall in price more dramatically than do short term bonds; these bonds are more susceptible to movements in interest rates. In addition, bonds that provide higher coupon payments will fluctuate less than bonds that pay lower coupon payments. Staggering the maturity dates of bonds, which mixes bonds with short, medium, and longer periods to maturity, as well as mixing the institutions issuing those bonds (to include governments and some corporate bonds) will allow you to build a diversified bond portfolio.

Bond trading is done between dealers, which means that you won't be able to view a complete auction market and its available quotes via the Internet or even the newspaper. These same dealers will be able to supply accurate calculations of bond yields and the current price. Some discount brokerages sell bonds with a face value as low as $1000, while the more typical minimum is $5000. Investors who invest in bonds directly as opposed to investing in bonds through a mutual fund will save on fees; saving 1/2 of 1 per cent can make a big difference to your net worth. Investors who want diversification and active management could consider a bond mutual fund that is offered by Altamira, C.I. CIBC, TD, or Trimark. All of these firms have earned an excellent reputation for their bond funds.

Upside Potential with Convertible Bonds

Tip 60

TO UNDERSTAND WHAT A CONVERTIBLE BOND IS, LETS REVIEW WHAT A BOND IS—AN INTEREST-BEARING INVESTMENT THAT OBLIGATES THE BORROWER TO PAY A SPECIFIC AMOUNT OF INTEREST FOR A SPECIFIC PERIOD OF TIME, AND THEN REPAY THE INVESTOR THE ORIGINAL AMOUNT OF THE LOAN.

Convertible bonds are bonds issued by corporations that are backed by the corporations' assets. In case of default, the bondholders have a legal claim on those assets. Convertible bonds are unique from other bonds or debt instruments because they give the holder of the bond the right, but not the obligation, to convert the bond into a predetermined number of shares of the issuing company. Therefore, the bonds combine the features of a bond with an "equity kicker"—if the stock price of the firm goes up the bondholder makes a lot of money (more than a traditional bondholder). If the stock price stays the same or declines, they receive interest payments and their principal payment, unlike the stock investor who lost money.

Why are convertible bonds worth considering? Convertible bonds have the potential for higher rates while providing investors with income on a regular basis. Consider the following:

- Convertible bonds offer regular interest payments, like regular bonds.

- Downturns in this investment category have not been as dramatic as in other investment categories.

- If the bond's underlying stock does decline in value, the minimum value of your investment will be equal to the value of a high yield bond. In short, the downside risk is a lot less than investing in the common stock directly. However, investors who purchase after a significant price appreciation should realize that the bond is "trading-off-the-common" which means they are no longer valued like a bond but rather like a stock. Therefore, the price could fluctuate significantly. The value of the bond is derived from the value of the underlying stock, and thus a decline in the value of the stock will also cause the bond to decline in value until it hits a floor that is the value of a traditional bond without the conversion.

- If the value of the underlying stock increases, bond investors can convert their bond holdings into stock and participate in the growth of the company.

During the past five years, convertible bonds have generated superior returns compared to more conservative bonds. Convertible bonds have generated higher returns because many companies have improved their financial performance and have had their stocks appreciate in value.

Convertible bonds can play an important role in a well-diversified investment portfolio for both conservative and aggressive investors. Investors who want to capitalize on the opportunities in convertible bonds do not have a lot of options in the Canadian market. Many mutual funds will invest a portion of their investments in convertible bonds, but no fund invests solely in convertible bonds. Investors who want to invest directly could consider a convertible bond from some of the largest companies in North America, including Rogers Communications.

Securing Your Return with Strip Bonds

Tip 61

IN THE INVESTMENT INDUSTRY YOU DEAL WITH A LOT OF ASSUMPTIONS: ABOUT VOLATILITY, RISK, GROWTH, RETURNS, AND QUALITY JUST TO NAME A FEW, BUT THERE IS ONE INVESTMENT THAT REQUIRES VERY FEW ASSUMPTIONS—STRIP BONDS. STRIP BONDS ARE AN INVESTMENT THAT IS GROWING IN POPULARITY IN CANADA. STRIP BONDS HAVE MANY FEATURES THAT MAKE THEM IDEALLY SUITED FOR INVESTORS WHO REQUIRE SECURE GROWTH AND STABILITY BUT WITH NO NEED FOR CURRENT INCOME.

Unlike some exotically named investment vehicles, here the name of the product says it all. First appearing in 1982 in Canada, these are typically high-quality government or quasi-government bonds, which have had their interest or coupons payments removed, or "stripped" away. Thus, a strip bond is a bond that pays no interest but gives you a large payment at maturity.

When interest payments are "stripped" from a bond two distinct investment products are created: the coupon (making up the group of interest-paying future-dated coupons) and the residual (the principal component of the bond). The bond residual is sold at a discount to its par value (below $1000) and matures at par ($1000). The difference between the discounted price at which you buy the bond residual and the par face value is the compounded return that you receive. The power of compound interest can lead to fairly steep discounts if there is a long time to maturity for either the bond or the coupon component.

Investors should consider these bonds because yields are higher than T-Bill rates, and with the wide variety of strip bonds that are available, maturity dates can be tailored for your investment objectives. The nature of the product itself leads to another advantage, namely the long-term guaranteed return available. Because there are no interest payments, as are made by regular bonds, there is no cash flow to be reinvested before maturity. Thus, there is no reinvestment risk, which comes from interest rate uncertainty when the coupon payments are received.

Aside from the credit risks inherent in all bonds, the major risk to strips is extreme price volatility. While the price of all bonds fluctuates according to market conditions, the longer the period till maturity for any bond, the greater will be the volatility. Even greater will be the volatility of a strip, compared to a bond of a similar interest and maturity date. A rise of a few percentage points in interest rates could easily chop the value of a long dated strip bond in half. Conservative investors find that this short-term volatility is irrelevant to their long-term time horizon. You are best to hold strips until maturity, which makes them convenient for a self-directed RRSP.

Aggressive investors may be inclined to try to profit from a strip bond's volatility, but a thin market and disadvantageous tax treatment make this difficult as you are still required to pay tax on the annual income earned, even if you don't receive it.

iUnits—For the Fee-Sensitive Investor

Tip 62

"CONSUMER BRANDING" IS THE BUZZWORD ON BAY STREET, WITH COMPANIES CHANGING THEIR CORPORATE IMAGE IN AN ATTEMPT TO IDENTIFY AND CREATE LOYALTY WITH THEIR CLIENTS. THUS, INVESTMENT PRODUCTS ARE GIVEN "POWER" NAMES, WITH MUTUAL FUNDS CALLED "AGGRESSIVE GROWTH," "EXCELSIOR," AND "DYNAMIC." AT THE OTHER END OF THE SPECTRUM IS A PRODUCT WITH AN UNCONVENTIONAL NAME FOR A VERY CONVENTIONAL INVESTMENT PRODUCT. THESE "IUNITS," WHICH IS SHORT FOR INDEX PARTICIPATION UNITS, ARE A NEW INVESTMENT VEHICLE LAUNCHED IN THE FALL OF 1999. THE I60 TYPE OF IUNITS MIRRORS THE RETURNS OF THE NEW MARKET INDEX, THE S&P/TSE 60. THE S&P/TSE 60 TRACKS THE PERFORMANCE OF 60 LARGE CANADIAN COMPANIES. INVESTORS PURCHASE A UNIT OF A TRUST. THE TRUST HOLDS THE STOCKS THAT ARE INCLUDED IN THE INDEX IN THE SAME PROPORTION AS THEY ARE REFLECTED IN THAT INDEX.

So far, this sounds like an index mutual fund in that investors can build a diversified portfolio without purchasing the shares in the 60 underlying companies. However, there are several important differences between iUnits and an index mutual fund that tracks the same index. Most notably, i60s trade just like any stock that is listed on the Toronto Stock Exchange. They have a symbol (XIU), and can be bought or sold at any time during the trading day, unlike mutual funds that have their prices set once a day. This means that you have to have a brokerage account, and will therefore pay a commission when you buy and when you sell. Also, just like stocks, you can buy iUnits on margin, which allows you to increase your returns if the units appreciate in value more than the interest rate you have to pay.

Probably the most important difference, as we face continued market uncertainty, is that iUnits can be sold short, subject to the same rules and regulations that apply to normal stocks. Thus, they give you a perfect opportunity to profit if the overall stock market declines. Finally, the ongoing management fees are very low. The manager of the units has contracted that the expenses of the fund will not exceed 0.17 per cent per year. This fee is roughly 75 per cent lower than the fees charged by some Canadian index mutual funds and 90 per cent lower than actively managed mutual funds.

Long-time investors will recognize that iUnits as similar to TIPs (a Toronto 35 Index Participation Fund that tracks the Toronto 35 Index) and HIPs (Toronto 100 Index Participation Fund that tracks the TSE 100 Index). In January 2000, TIPs and HIPs were merged into i60s, with the only difference being that there are now fees associated with the units. Previously, the Toronto Stock Exchange subsidized the operational costs of TIPs and HIPs.

As with any passive investment, you can't expect to beat the market, but merely to equal it. When markets fall, the value of your iUnits will drop right along with it. For investors who require further information check the web site at www.iunits.com or call 1-877-464-8648.

Spiders and Diamonds—
Not Just Bugs and Rocks

Tip 63

THERE IS MORE THAN ONE STOCK EXCHANGE AND WITH MORE THAN ONE

STOCK EXCHANGE THERE IS COMPETITION BETWEEN THESE ORGANIZATIONS.

THEY COMPETE FOR COMPANIES TO LIST THEIR SHARES ON THEIR EXCHANGE,

AND TO CREATE PRODUCTS THAT WILL BE ACTIVELY TRADED, AND THUS

GARNER VOLUME, INTEREST, AND PROFITS. THE AMERICAN STOCK EXCHANGE,

OR AMEX, (PART OF THE NASDAQ) HAS, ARGUABLY, BEEN THE MOST AGGRESSIVE

IN THIS ARENA, CREATING SOME PRODUCTS THAT SHOULD BE OF INTEREST TO

A WIDER RANGE OF INVESTORS.

The Amex has produced products that are all basically indexed investment vehicles. Very similar to iUnits in Canada, these products allow for the tracking of various indices in exchange-traded products. However, the range of products offered in the much larger U.S. market allows for much broader diversification for some products or a much narrower focus for other products than here in Canada.

Much like iUnits, these products are traded like stocks but offer the diversification of an index mutual fund. They are bought and sold on the Amex, which means that you will need a Canadian brokerage account (all Canadian brokers can handle orders on the Amex, though at prices moderately higher than the Toronto Stock Exchange). Like stocks they can be bought or sold at any time during the trading day, can be margined, and can be sold short.

Here come the acronyms for some of the products that are available:

- SPDRs, known as Spiders, are short for Standard & Poor's Depository Receipts, and are based on the very broad index the S&P 500. This is the favourite index of most institutional investors, as it is much more diversified than the better-known Dow Jones 30. SPDRs are a perfect way to get exposure to the U.S. market.

- MidCap SPDRs, are very similar to their larger cousins above, and track the Standard & Poor's 400 Mid-Cap Index of U.S. companies, which are not large enough to make it into the S&P 500.

- Nasdaq-100 Index Tracking Stocks follow the largest companies traded on the NASDAQ.

- Select Sector SPDRs were created at the end of 1998, and offer an index exposure to each of the nine major sectors of the S&P 500. These include basic industries, consumer services, consumer staples, cyclicals and transportation, energy, financial, industrial, technology, and utilities. They allow you to focus on a particular U.S. market sector.

- DIAMONDS are based on the well-known Dow Jones Industrial Average, offering tracking exposure to the 30 largest companies in the U.S.

As with iUnits, annual expenses are much lower than for index mutual funds—under 0.30 per cent annually. And again, it should be remembered that indexing on its own is no panacea: markets of all types can fall as well as rise. But these products help diversify portfolios and offer exposure to the powerhouse U.S. stock market. For more information check the web site of the American Stock Exchange at www.amex.com.

WEBS—Weaving the World Together

Tip 64

EVERY MONTH THE FINANCIAL SERVICES INDUSTRY INTRODUCES NEW MUTUAL FUNDS THAT ARE DESIGNED TO ATTRACT INVESTORS' ATTENTION AND MONEY. THE UNIVERSE OF INDEX PRODUCTS THAT ARE TRADED ON STOCK EXCHANGES HAS NOW ALSO EXPANDED TO INCLUDE THE INDEXES OF OTHER COUNTRIES. WORLD EQUITY BENCHMARK SHARES (WEBS) ARE PASSIVELY MANAGED, INDEX-BASED INVESTMENTS FOR 17 COUNTRIES AROUND THE WORLD. EACH OF THE 17 COUNTRIES HAS ITS OWN WEBS. EACH WEBS HOLDS A DIVERSIFIED PORTFOLIO OF STOCKS FROM ITS RESPECTIVE FOREIGN COUNTRY.

They are similar to other investment vehicles like the iUnits, SPDRs, and DIAMONDS discussed in the media on an almost daily basis. They trade just as stocks do on the American Stock Exchange. However, they offer entrance to some interesting global markets that are typically inaccessible to most individual investors. A country WEBS is attractive because it is a low cost and diversified investment vehicle that has the potential to generate good rates of return with a low probability of underperformance.

For example, the Canada WEBs is based on the Morgan Stanley Capital International Inc. (MSCI) Canada Index, which consists of 78 stocks that are primarily traded on the

Toronto Stock Exchange, including Northern Telecom, BCE Inc., and Thomson Corp. However, investors will likely find other country's WEBS more appealing than the Canada WEBS. WEBS are available for various countries, such as Australia, France, Germany, Japan, Malaysia, Singapore and Spain. They are typically almost fully invested in the stocks that make up the underlying country's index. Thus, investors can quickly gain exposure to a country by investing in a country's WEBS.

You can invest in a WEB through a stock or discount broker. They are marginable, and can be sold short, even on the downtick (a selling short convention). Unlike other Amex products, but similar to mutual funds, WEBS are valued daily, based on local market closing prices. As of the end of 1998, WEBS, like SPDRs and DIAMONDS, are considered to be qualified investments for an RRSP, though they are considered to be foreign property.

While WEBS make trading in foreign stocks a whole lot easier, they do not remove the risks associated with in various stock markets. WEBS trade in U.S. Dollars, but investors still have foreign currency exposure because WEBS do not hedge their foreign currency exposure. Some emerging country WEBS are highly volatile, a fact that is fully reflected in the price of a country's WEBS. In addition, some of these WEBS may trade at a small discount or premium although there is a continuous creation/redemption process of shares at the net asset value which should reduce this divergence.

Considering the performance of some of these countries and the inability for investors to place money in a mutual fund that invests in these countries, a WEBS becomes a very attractive investment. Aggressive investors who prefer to keep the management fee in their pocket should seriously consider WEBS in order to gain exposure to global equity markets.

You can find more information at www.websontheweb.com or www.amex.com.

Lowering Your Tax
with Dividend-Paying Stocks

Tip 65

CANADIAN COMPANIES HAVE TO PAY THEIR DIVIDENDS WITH AFTER-TAX DOLLARS. THIS MEANS THAT COMPANIES THAT EARN A PROFIT PAY TAXES, AND WHATEVER MONEY IS LEFT OVER IS EITHER REINVESTED IN THE COMPANY OR PAID TO SHAREHOLDERS IN THE FORM OF A DIVIDEND. ONCE INVESTORS RECEIVE THE DIVIDEND THEY HAVE TO PAY TAXES AGAIN ON THIS DIVIDEND. IN ORDER TO REDUCE THIS "DOUBLE TAXATION," A DIVIDEND TAX CREDIT IS PROVIDED TO CANADIAN TAXPAYERS, THEREBY REDUCING THEIR TAX LIABILITY AND INCREASING THEIR INVESTMENT RETURN.

Dividend and interest income are therefore not treated equally. The following table compares the after-tax return of an investment that generates a before-tax return of 10 per cent. An investor who is in the lowest tax bracket and invested in a fixed income investment would earn an after-tax rate of return of 7.3 per cent. However, if that same investor invested in a dividend paying stock that earned a before-tax return of 10 per cent, their after tax rate of return would have been 9.2 per cent.

TAXABLE INCOME BRACKETS	COMBINED FEDERAL AND PROVINCIAL TAX RATE*	AFTER-TAX YIELD ON A 10 PER CENT INVESTMENT	
		Interest	Dividend
$30,004 or less	26%	7.3%	9.2%
Between $30,004 and $60,009	40%	5.9%	7.5%
$60,009 and over	45%	5.5%	6.9%

*Assumes a surtax of 3 per cent and a provincial tax rate of 50 per cent

Why else are dividends important? In the United States a study based on the companies that comprise the Dow Jones Industrial Average index ranked these 30 stocks by dividend yield. Over a long period of time a portfolio of stocks that had the highest dividend yield also generated the best return. Thus, investors who favour dividend-paying stocks over the long-term earned a higher rate of return.

Most investments that have a high dividend yield are real estate companies or unit investment trusts, but conservative investors wondering where to place the portion of their equity portfolio dedicated to equities could consider investing in good blue chip stocks that pay a reasonable dividend yield. Investors should diversify their portfolio in order to avoid another TransCanada Pipeline scenario—a big blue chip company that recently reduced its dividend and thereby its share price. The following is a list of some of Canada's largest blue chip companies that should continue to generate good dividend growth along with capital appreciation.

TICKER	NAME	DIVIDEND YIELD	DIVIDEND	STYLE
AL	Alcan Aluminium Ltd.	1.9%	$ 0.88	Value
BNS	Bank of Nova Scotia	2.7%	$ 0.90	Value
BCE	BCE Inc.	1.8%	$ 1.36	Growth
BTS	BCT.TELUS Comm.	4.0%	$ 1.40	Value
IMO	Imperial Oil Limited	2.6%	$ 0.76	Value
RY	Royal Bank of Canada	2.7%	$ 1.96	Value
SHC	Shell Canada Ltd., A	2.6%	$ 0.72	Value
TOC	Thomson Corporation	2.3%	$ 0.98	Growth
TD	Toronto-Dominion Bank	2.3%	$ 0.59	Value

As at April 30, 2000

Note that the dividend yield will vary depending on the stock price.

Blue Chip Stocks—Not a Poker Game

Tip 66

INVESTING IN CONSERVATIVE BLUE CHIP STOCKS MAY NOT HAVE THE ALLURE OF A HOT HIGH-TECH INVESTMENT, BUT IT CAN BE HIGHLY REWARDING NONETHE-LESS, AS GOOD QUALITY STOCKS HAVE OUTPERFORMED OTHER INVESTMENT CLASSES OVER THE LONG TERM.

Historically, investing in stocks has generated a return, over time, of between 11 and 15 per cent annually depending how aggressive you are. Stocks outperform other investments since they incur more risk. Stock investors are at the bottom of the corporate "food chain." First, companies have to pay their employees and suppliers. Then they pay their bond-holders. After this come the preferred shareholders. Companies have an obligation to pay all of these stakeholders first, and if there is money leftover it is paid to the stockholders through dividends or retained earnings. Sometimes there is a lot of money left over for stockholders, and in other cases there isn't. Thus, investing in stocks is risky because investors never know exactly what they are going to receive for their investment.

What are the attractions of blue chip stocks?

- Great long-term rates of return.

- Unlike mutual funds, another relatively safe, long term investment category, there are no ongoing fees.

- You become an owner of a company.

So much for the benefits—what about the risks?

- Some investors can't tolerate both the risk associated with investing in the stock market and the risk associated with investing in one company. Not all blue chips are created equal.

- If you don't have the time and skill to identify a good quality company at a fair price don't invest directly. Rather, you should consider a good mutual fund.

Selecting a blue chip company is only part of the battle—determining the appropriate price is the other. Theoretically, the value of a stock is the present value of all future cash flows discounted at the appropriate discount rate. However, like most theoretical answers, this doesn't fully explain reality. In reality supply and demand for a stock sets the stock's daily price, and demand for a stock will increase or decrease depending of the outlook for a company. Thus, stock prices are driven by investor expectations for a company, the more favourable the expectations the better the stock price. In short, the stock market is a voting machine and much of the time it is voting based on investors' fear or greed, not on their rational assessments of value. Stock prices can swing widely in the short-term but they eventually converge to their intrinsic value over the long-term.

Investors should look at good companies with great expectations that are not yet imbedded in the price of a stock. You may want to consider some of the following Canadian blue chip companies: Alcan Aluminium Ltd., Bank of Montreal, Bank of Nova Scotia, Barrick Gold Corp., BCE Inc., BCT.TELUS, Bombardier Inc, Celestica Inc., Imperial Oil Ltd., JDS Uniphase, Loblaw Companies Ltd., Nortel Networks, Research in Motion, Royal Bank of Canada, Seagram Company Ltd., Thomson Corp., and Toronto-Dominion Bank.

Life Insurance as an Investment

Tip 67

TERM INSURANCE PROVIDES COVERAGE FOR A PRE-SPECIFIED PERIOD. FOR EXAMPLE, TERM INSURANCE IS DESIGNED TO PROTECT A MORTGAGE OR PROVIDE INCOME FOR YOUR FAMILY IN CASE OF YOUR DEATH. YOU PAY THE TERM INSURANCE PREMIUM EACH MONTH AND AS LONG AS YOU PAY THE PREMIUM YOUR POLICY WILL STAY IN FORCE. ONCE THE CONTRACT REACHES MATURITY (USUALLY IN 10 YEARS) YOU NEED TO RENEW YOUR POLICY AT A HIGHER PRICE. IF YOU DIE WHILE YOU'RE PAYING THE PREMIUM YOUR ESTATE GETS A LARGE SUM OF MONEY.

In contrast, permanent or whole life insurance remains in force until you die. You pay the premium on a monthly basis for a pre-specified term, which can range between 10 to 20 years. A portion of your monthly payment pays the insurance and the life insurance company that provided the insurance invests the remainder. Eventually you don't pay any premiums but your estate still receives a large payment upon death.

Whole life policies have been criticized because their investment returns are low. Thus you were often advised to buy life insurance protection with a term policy and invest the difference between term and whole life payments in a separate investment vehicle, such as mutual funds, stocks, or bonds. Once you have built up a large pool of assets you don't need the insurance because the assets will provide security and stability in the event of an unexpected death.

However, there is a new, more flexible product called universal life insurance. While the life insurance company controls the savings in a whole life policy, the savings in a universal life plan are owned and controlled by the policyholder. Insurance companies offer a large variety of investment options for this savings component, including mutual funds. Thus, you have the ability to meet your life insurance needs and increase your return on investment.

The major advantage of a universal life policy is tax-advantaged growth. When you pay the policy premium, a portion of the premium pays for the insurance and a portion is invested. However, when you are ready to withdraw the money from your investment, your cost basis (the portion not subject to tax) is higher with a universal life policy. The cost base for a universal policy is equal to the sum of all your premiums—the amount of money you have invested plus the money you have used to buy life insurance. This is very useful because increasing your cost base will ensure you pay less tax once you sell your investments within the universal life policy.

Universal life insurance provides a powerful combination of life insurance and tax-advantaged investment opportunities. Investors should realize that universal life insurance premiums work twice as hard as other premiums. They should also know that choosing the right product is an important element in the overall success of this strategy. Finally, the benefits of this strategy are magnified if you are in a higher tax bracket and have maximized your RRSP contribution.

Got $150 000? Consider a Pooled Fund

Tip 68

SOMETIMES COMPANIES HAVE THE ABILITY TO CHARGE DIFFERENT PRICES TO DIFFERENT PEOPLE FOR ROUGHLY THE SAME PRODUCTS AND SERVICES. CONSUMERS WHO PAY THE LOWER COST WILL RECEIVE FEWER BELLS AND WHISTLES, BUT THE CORE PRODUCT OR SERVICE IS THE SAME. EXAMPLES OF THIS STRATEGY INCLUDE THE DIFFERENT PRICES FOR AIRLINE SEATS ON THE SAME FLIGHT, OUTLET STORES THAT SELL DISCOUNTED MERCHANDISE, OR CHEAPER WEEKDAY NIGHTS AT THE MOVIES. IN THE INVESTMENT INDUSTRY, THIS SAME DIFFERENCE IN PRICING IS FOUND WITH POOLED FUNDS. POOLED FUNDS ARE ALMOST LIKE A MUTUAL FUND—THEY GROUP TOGETHER THE MONEY FROM INDIVIDUAL INVESTORS AND AIM TO PROVIDE THESE INVESTORS WITH A GOOD RATE OF RETURN GIVEN THE OBJECTIVE OF THE FUND. HOWEVER, INVESTORS WHO INVEST IN A POOLED FUND WILL BENEFIT FROM LOWER MANAGEMENT FEES DUE TO THE LARGE INVESTMENT REQUIRED.

Like a mutual fund a pooled fund is a "pool" of investors' savings. Investors who want to invest in Canadian equities pool their money into one fund, another fund for money market investments, yet another for a balanced mandate. Like a mutual fund, the pooled fund provides a number of benefits for investors including professional management, diversification, convenience, and liquidity for easy access and withdrawal.

While pooled funds and mutual funds are very similar, there are a few differences:

- Pooled funds charge lower management fees.

- Pooled funds are typically available only to members of company- or group-sponsored plans, while mutual funds are usually available to both individual investors and company- or group-sponsored plans.

- Investors who do not belong to company- or group-sponsored plans usually have to invest at least $150 000 in a pooled fund.

- Pooled fund investors have more access to the investment management company and receive a higher level of service.

Since the performance between pooled funds and mutual funds before any management fees is very similar, investors should be very conscious of the management fee charged. The size of this fee can make a large difference to their net worth. For example, assume there are two funds: a pooled fund and a mutual fund, and both generated a return of 12 per cent per year before any fees were deducted. The mutual fund has a management expense ratio of 2 per cent, while the pooled fund has a management expense ratio of 1 per cent. The investor who invested $1 000 000 in the pooled fund will have an additional $245 680, or 9.47 per cent in her investment after 10 years because they paid $151 530 less in management expenses during that same 10-year time frame. Thus, a large investment, a long time horizon, and a lower management fee equals big money in your pocket. If you have $150 000 of investments you should consider a good pooled fund and what it can do for you.

Ask your current mutual fund provider if they provide pooled funds. Companies like Bissett, Sceptre, and TAL Private Management offer pooled funds.

A Higher Income with Real Estate Investment Trusts

Tip 69

WHILE THE LIST OF WHAT IS AN ALLOWABLE INVESTMENT IN AN RRSP IS QUITE BROAD, THE DOOR SLAMS SHUT WHEN IT COMES TO REAL ESTATE. NEITHER COMMERCIAL NOR RESIDENTIAL BUILDINGS ARE ALLOWED, AND NEITHER IS RAW LAND. WHAT IS ALLOWED IN AN RRSP ARE SHARES OF CANADIAN REAL ESTATE COMPANIES, OR REAL ESTATE INVESTMENT TRUSTS (REITS). CONSERVATIVE INVESTORS WHO WANT TO INVEST IN REAL ESTATE SHOULD CONSIDER REITS BECAUSE THEY PROVIDE INCOME, LIQUIDITY, AND GROWTH POTENTIAL.

REITs are traded on stock exchanges and are structured as trusts, which acquire full or partial ownership of revenue-producing real estate. In turn, the trust then issues shares in this venture, which are listed on stock exchanges in Canada or the United States, like a closed end mutual fund. The attraction for investors is that revenues flow through to the shareholders or investors net of management fees or expenses. REITs may hold a wide variety of real estate, including shopping centres, office buildings, industrial buildings, hotels, and multi-unit residential structures. The real estate is predominantly income-producing property, not raw land.

Investors include the amount of net income received from the REIT when calculating their income for tax purposes, but a portion of the income is treated as a return of capital, which reduces the investor's cost base for income tax purposes (i.e., REITs provide a higher after-tax return).

REITs also offer the following benefits:

- REITs are a diversified portfolio of properties.

- There is liquidity—you can easily buy and sell securities on a regular and timely basis.

- REITs have a debt limit of about 50 per cent of shareholder equity, and thus avoid the potential negative problems that come with leverage.

- The REIT market in the United States is very well developed, with over 300 REITs with assets of over US$130 billion. The Canadian market is much younger. The first REIT was introduced in 1993, and the market has since grown to 12 REITs. Total market capitalization is around $4 billion.

However, there are some problems with REITs. The small size of the market here presents a more limited menu of choices than in the U.S. Specialized REITs are available south of the border that concentrate on properties such as nursing home properties, storage facilities, or jails. REITs have also underperformed the overall market in both countries, following the general lacklustre returns of the real estate industry.

REITs typically pay a steady dividend, which at today's levels is relatively high. Low leverage and prudent management helps to keep this steady income flow, compared to returns from direct ownership of real estate stocks. The following is a list of REITs that you could consider for your investment portfolio:

TICKER	NAME	DIVIDEND YIELD	DIVIDEND	STYLE
RYL.U	Royal Host REIT	16.0%	$ 1.08	Growth
LGY.U	Legacy Hotels REIT	11.2%	$ 0.69	Value
MRT.U	Morguard REIT	11.2%	$ 0.90	Value
REI.U	RioCan REIT	11.1%	$ 0.97	Value
REF.U	Cdn. REIT	10.2%	$ 1.07	Value
HR.U	H&R REIT	9.9%	$ 1.01	Value
CPL.U	CPL Long Term Care REIT	8.0%	$ 1.49	Growth

Uncommon Returns with Royalty Trusts

Tip 70

DURING THE 1980S, WHEN INTEREST RATES WERE NEARLY 20 PER CENT, SEEKING HIGHER RETURN ALTERNATIVES WAS NOT A BIG PRIORITY. NOW, WITH INTEREST RATES LESS THAN HALF OF THOSE LEVELS, EVERY EXTRA PER CENT CAN MAKE A VERY BIG DIFFERENCE TO AN INVESTOR'S ANNUAL CASH FLOW. A NEW INVEST-MENT ALTERNATIVE PROVIDING RELATIVELY HIGH INTEREST RATES IS A ROYALTY TRUST. OPERATING IN A VERY SIMILAR WAY TO A REIT, ROYALTY TRUSTS ARE "TRUSTS" THAT TAKE OWNERSHIP OF INCOME-PRODUCING ASSETS, AND WHICH IN TURN SELL SHARES TO THE PUBLIC. WHILE THEY HAVE BEEN A HOT ITEM IN THE PAST FEW YEARS, TORONTO STOCK EXCHANGE-LISTED INCOME OR ROYALTY TRUSTS DATE BACK TO THE 1970S. CURRENTLY THERE ARE MORE THAN 70 SUCH TRUSTS, WITH A TOTAL MARKET CAPITALIZATION OF OVER $15 BILLION.

The assets that are owned vary widely from trust to trust. The oldest form of trust owns a commodity-based product such as petroleum or coal. The asset being invested in affects the revenue stream, which flows through to investors. Many of these trusts make returns of capital to investors in a way similar to REITs (see Tip 69). These distributions result in a lower cost base for investors and in turn, higher after-tax rates of return. Others have more typical interest returns to investors.

The appeal of royalty trusts is based on the yields obtained, which are usually much higher than GICs. However, it is important to remember that there are considerably higher risks associated with investing in royalty trusts. In all cases, income distributions are tied to the values of the underlying assets. Investors should remember that a distribution sometimes includes a return of capital, which makes the reported yield somewhat inflated.

The risks of royalty trusts have been evident in the past few years, as many commodity prices fell, despite the predictions of some forecasters. If the price of oil, or gas, or whatever the basic asset owned by the trust falls, so will your return. Royalty trusts are not immune from the typical impact of business cycles, exchange rate fluctuations, and all of the other forces that affect prices for shares traded on exchanges.

Assessing the impact of these risks is made all the more difficult given that the actual assets owned will vary from trust to trust. Thus, it is important to invest in a combination of these investments in conjunction with other assets.

As with any investment, look beyond the current yield and simple comparisons to GICs and consider whether you are willing to accept the risks associated with the trust's underlying assets. The following is a partial list of some royalty trusts that you may want to consider.

TICKER	NAME	DIVIDEND YIELD	DIVIDEND	STYLE
NCF.U	NCE Petrofund	18.8%	$ 0.71	Value
PGF.U	Pengrowth Energy Trust	16.9%	$ 2.51	Growth
RSI.U	Rogers Sugar Inc Fund	11.2%	$ 0.57	Growth
SPF.U	Superior Propane	10.2%	$ 0.99	Value
TPL.U	TransCanada Power,L.P.	8.6%	$ 1.77	Growth

Getting in on an Initial Public Offering

Tip 71

DURING BULL MARKETS INVESTORS CLAMOUR FOR ACCESS TO INITIAL PUBLIC OFFERINGS (IPOS), WHICH REPRESENTS A COMPANY'S FIRST SALE OF STOCK TO THE PUBLIC. WITH RECENT STORIES OF HIGH-TECH FIRMS THAT GO PUBLIC AND SEE THEIR STOCKS DOUBLE OR TRIPLE ON THE FIRST DAY, IT'S EASY TO SEE WHY INVESTORS WANT TO PARTICIPATE. HOWEVER, IT IS WORTHWHILE TO STEP BACK AND LOOK AT THE LONGER-TERM PERFORMANCE OF SUCH STOCK OFFERINGS, AND PERHAPS QUESTION WHETHER YOU SHOULD SPEND MUCH OF YOUR ENERGY IN SEEKING OUT IPOS.

First some mechanics. A company that wishes to have its shares trade on an exchange hires an investment house to act as an underwriter. The underwriter sells shares to a group of initial buyers at a fixed price. The company determines the price with the guidance of the underwriter. The process of determining a price is both art and science. Setting the price too high would cause the price to fall when the shares trade on an exchange, a process which is bad for both the company's and the underwriter's reputation. On the other hand, pricing too low results in the company not receiving the full amount of money that it could have otherwise received. In practice, prices are typically set near, but somewhat below what is determined to be the market price, hence the reason why many IPOs jump in value on the first day of trading.

Getting your hands on an IPO is a major issue for smaller investors, who often find that they have access to only the shares allocated to the brokerage firm that they use. Thus, a firm's access to IPOs is one factor that you can use to choose a brokerage firm.

In examining IPO performance there are two issues: the amount of underpricing, (the difference between the issue price and the price immediately after the stock starts trading) and the long-term price performance of the IPO. Vijay Jog, a professor of finance at the School of Business, Carleton University, has reported that underpricing in the Canadian marketplace has been approximately 8 per cent, from 1971 to 1995. In the longer term a pattern of positive average initial returns followed by an extended period of strongly negative returns develops. In his work examining Canadian price performance during the 1975 to 1994 period, he determined that while investment in an average IPO has appreciated, adjusting the returns for the underlying benchmark shows a high degree of negative returns, duplicating results found in the United States.

Thus, a simple buy and hold strategy may yield inferior results, as the average IPO appears to perform well below the benchmark. While there is an initial amount of under pricing, the overall performance is below the benchmark within a year of the IPO. Investors should adjust their strategies accordingly.

Increasing Your
Investment Options with Options

Tip 72

THE WORLD OF OPTIONS CAN BE QUITE COMPLEX. HOWEVER, WITH THIS

COMPLEXITY COMES OPPORTUNITY, AS YOU CAN USE OPTIONS TO SUIT YOUR

OWN RISK AND RETURN CHARACTERISTICS. YOU CAN, FOR EXAMPLE, EMPLOY A

CONSERVATIVE STRATEGY IN ORDER TO GENERATE EXTRA INCOME AND

REDUCE THE RISK ASSOCIATED WITH INVESTMENTS THAT YOU ALREADY HOLD.

An option is a contract with a specified expiration date that gives the right either to buy (a "call option") or to sell (a "put option") a specified amount of a particular asset at a fixed price. It permits this purchase or sale; it does not necessitate it. In short, an option gives you the option to either buy or sell an asset at a predefined price on a predefined date.

Options have value, or premium, and you can either sell or purchase this value depending on your strategy. Option buyers pay a premium to option sellers (or "writers") to obtain an option.

Option use is limitless, but here is one use. One of the most conservative option strategies is called covered call writing, where an investor who owns a particular stock writes (sells) a call option against a stock that is already owned. Here is the example. An individual owns 100 shares of Bank of Montreal (BMO) stock at $30. The same investor could write a call option on these same shares at an exercise price of $35, and receive a premium of $1. Therefore, today the writer receives, before commissions, the premium of $100 (a $1 premium multiplied by 100 shares). This then immediately lowers the cost of each share purchased to $29. If, by the time the option is exercised, BMO stock is trading at more than $35, your shares will be "called away" and you will be paid the $35 per share that you are obligated to sell. Therefore, at any price above $35, your gain will be $5 on the stock and $1 for the premium, for a total gain of $6. Should BMO fail to rise beyond $35, you will retain the $1 per share premium, as well as the stock that you have owned all along.

Covered call writing is considered to be conservative in that the worst that will happen is that you will have to give up the underlying asset, in this case the stock of BMO. The calls are thus "covered" or protected by the ownership of the underlying stock.

This strategy is based on the belief that stocks don't rise dramatically every day and that more frequently an investor applying this strategy will retain both their stock and the premium that was generated; only about 11 per cent of stocks are "called-away" over time. Sophisticated investors should consider the merits of this strategy or other strategies that can be utilized when investing in options.

Hedge Funds—
Establishing a New Frontier

Tip 73

IT IS DIFFICULT TO PROVIDE A GENERAL DEFINITION OF A HEDGE FUND. INITIALLY, HEDGE FUNDS WOULD SELL SHORT THE STOCK MARKET, THUS PROVIDING A "HEDGE" AGAINST ANY STOCK MARKET DECLINES. TODAY THE TERM IS APPLIED MORE BROADLY TO ANY TYPE OF PRIVATE INVESTMENT PARTNERSHIP. THERE ARE THOUSANDS OF DIFFERENT HEDGE FUNDS GLOBALLY, ALTHOUGH THERE ARE VERY FEW IN CANADA. THEIR PRIMARY OBJECTIVE IS TO MAKE LOTS OF MONEY, AND TO MAKE MONEY BY INVESTING IN ALL SORTS OF DIFFERENT INVESTMENTS AND INVESTMENTS STRATEGIES. MOST OF THESE STRATEGIES ARE MORE AGGRESSIVE THAN THE INVESTMENTS MADE BY MUTUAL FUNDS.

A hedge fund is thus a private investment fund, which invests in a variety of different investments. The general partner chooses the different investments and also handles all of the trading activity and day-to-day operations of the fund. The investor or the limited partners invest most of the money and participate in the gains of the fund. The general manager usually charges a small management fee and a large incentive bonus if they earn a high rate of return.

While this may sound a lot like a mutual fund, there are major differences:

- Mutual funds are operated by mutual fund or investment companies and are heavily regulated. Hedge funds, as private funds, have far fewer restrictions and regulations.

- Mutual fund companies invest their client's money, while hedge funds invest their client's money and their own money in the underlying investments.

- Hedge funds charge a performance bonus: usually 20 per cent of all the gains above a certain hurdle rate, which is in line with equity market returns. Some hedge funds have been able to generate annual rates of return of 50 per cent or more, even during difficult market environments.

- Mutual funds have disclosure and other requirements that prohibit a fund from investing in derivative products, using leverage, short selling, taking too large a position in one investment, or investing in commodities. Hedge funds are free to invest however they wish.

Hedge funds are not permitted to solicit investments, which is likely why you hear very little about these funds. During the previous five years some of these funds have doubled, tripled, quadrupled in value or more. However, hedge funds do incur large risks and just as many funds have disappeared after losing big. Long-term investors may wish to examine hedge funds, keeping in mind that most require a minimum investment of $150 000 in Ontario. This minimum requirement allows hedge funds to retain their investment flexibility and generate superior returns for investors. The most popular hedge fund in Canada was the BPI Global Opportunities Fund. However, this fund attracted more than $1 billion of investors' money and is now closed to new investors. C.I. Mutual Funds also offers similar products. Investors could also consider the Goodwood Fund. Some hedge funds are also traded on the stock exchange, and include hedge funds run by Newcastle and YMG Capital.

No Money Down with Futures

Tip 74

THE FUTURES MARKET OFFERS THE OPPORTUNISTIC INVESTOR THE OPTION OF USING SMALL AMOUNTS OF THEIR OWN MONEY TO CONTROL LARGE AMOUNTS OF PRODUCTS, INCLUDING GOLD, CURRENCIES, AND AGRICULTURAL COMMODITIES.

A futures contract is a legally binding contract to deliver, if you are selling, or to take delivery, if you are buying, of a specific commodity, index, bond, or currency at a predetermined date or price. A futures contract can include everything from a standard size amount of wheat, oil, or a country's currency. The amount and date of delivery of the contract are specified, though in almost all cases delivery is not taken as contracts are bought and sold for speculative or hedging purposes.

Futures are utilized by both those who use the actual commodity and by investors. For example, in May a farmer plants some corn, but doesn't know what corn will be selling for in November. He can sell a futures contract for November and "lock in" the future selling price today. On the other hand investors can buy a futures contract if they believe the price of a security is going to appreciate, or they can sell a futures contract if they believe the price of a security is going to decline.

Futures are often thought of in the same category as options. While they are both derivatives, in that they derive their value from some base security, there is one very important difference. While options give the right, but not the obligation to buy or sell the underlying security, a futures contract is a legally binding obligation to buy or sell that same commodity. Thus, while options limit your loss to the price paid for that option, futures trading could lead to a loss of your entire investment and more to meet that obligation.

Another difference between the futures and the equities markets involves the use of the word margin. Although the contract sizes for currencies are large (often the equivalent of over $100 000 for a single contract), an investor does not have to buy or sell a full contract. Rather, a margin deposit on the contract is maintained, which is actually a "good faith" amount of money to ensure your obligations to the full amount of the futures contact. Minimum margin requirements vary by broker, but are typically only a fraction of the contract's total value, and are not related to the actual price of the contract involved.

Futures trades must be made through futures brokers, who operate both full-service and discount operations, and may be related to the stock brokerage that you already deal with. However, popular discount stockbrokers, such as TD Waterhouse, do not handle futures contracts. Most futures dealers are U.S.-based, but will open accounts for Canadian customers. Futures of all types, including financial and commodity futures, cannot be held in an RRSP.

Eight

The Stock Marketplace

The stock market is the place where investors and companies meet to exchange a portion of a company for capital or money. Investors who have money to invest and companies that need money to grow their business exchange their commodities through the stock exchange. This is the basis for the stock market—it is not a casino, but it does contain risks. Companies have no obligation to make money for their investors. However, investors as a group do require higher rates of return to reduce the risk associated with investing in these securities.

Investing in stocks is wise; study after study has concluded that stocks outperform every other major investment category over the long term. While investors should diversify their investments, most investors should have a portion of their portfolio invested in the stock market in one form or another. Conservative investors should invest in a mutual fund, while more aggressive investors could invest in either mutual funds or directly in stocks.

The growing trend in the past decade has been towards more direct ownership of stocks by investors of all types. Therefore, this chapter begins with the all-important task of finding a good discount broker for those investors who are confident that they can make their own investment decisions. There are many advantages to discount brokers, primarily involving far lower costs, while the biggest limitation is the lack of advice. Then we cover tips to help all investors by highlighting how to execute your trading orders better. Stock markets are volatile but individual stocks are even more volatile, with some stocks rising or falling by more than 10 or 20 per cent on one day with no rational explanation. Knowing how to buy or sell these investments, as well as less volatile investments, will help ensure that you can buy your investments at the prices that you want.

We also discuss the merits of investment clubs, where you get to share your investment ideas, learn about investments, and get exposure to alternative points of view. We also discuss various investment anomalies that are present in the (largely efficient) stock market. These little tricks of the trade can be used to increase your investment returns in the stocks that you purchase. These tips include how stock markets act at various times of the day, week, and month. In addition, we review what firm-specific characteristics are important to overall investment returns, which in turn can be used to search for and identify attractive investments.

We also explain the differences between value and growth investing, the two main approaches to picking stocks. This is not an academic exercise, as these investment styles are some of the biggest determinates of a stock's short-term performance. We also examine alternative investment styles, including the hot topic of momentum investing, and show you how you can profit from investments that decline in value. Finally we finish the chapter highlighting when you should consider selling your investments.

Finding the Best Discount Broker

Tip 75

ACCORDING TO THE TORONTO CONSULTING FIRM INVESTOR ECONOMICS INC., CANADIAN INVESTORS HAVE INVESTED MORE THAN $62 BILLION IN DISCOUNT BROKERAGE ACCOUNTS. THIS DO-IT-YOURSELF CROWD IS GAINING CONVERTS ON A DAILY BASIS, TO SUCH A DEGREE THAT MANY DISCOUNT BROKERAGE FIRMS ARE HAVING A VERY DIFFICULT TIME DEALING WITH THE INCREASED TRADING VOLUME. AT SOME DISCOUNT BROKERAGE HOUSES THE WAITING TIME DURING PEAK PERIODS HAS BEEN GREATER THAN ONE HOUR BEFORE YOU COULD SPEAK WITH A REPRESENTATIVE. WHILE THESE COMPANIES ARE CONTINUING TO TRAIN NEW STAFF, ADAPTING TO THIS NEW POPULARITY TAKES TIME.

Last year *Canadian Business* magazine conducted a review of the major discount brokerage houses and rated their services. Here is a summary of the results.

FIRM	CANADIAN BUSINESS RATING
TD Waterhouse	A-
Royal Bank Action Direct	B+
Bank of Montreal InvestorLine	B+
Charles Schwab Canada	B
E*Trade Canada	C+
HSBC InvestDirect	C
CIBC Investor's Edge	C
Sun Life Securities	C-
National Bank InvesTel	D+
Scotia Discount Brokerage	D

Firms were rated comparing cost, online trading availability, touch-tone trading, product selection, mutual funds, response time, the user experience, and extra services available. Interestingly, while overall ratings varied widely, most of these discount firms charged the same cost per trade. If you invested $10 000 in an average-priced stock, most firms would charge you between $25 and $30—a big difference from a full service broker who would charge at least $100. To connect with these firms contact:

FIRM	INTERNET ADDRESS	TELEPHONE
TD Waterhouse	www.tdwaterhouse.ca	1-800-659-7553
Royal Bank Action Direct	www.actiondirect.com	1-800-ROYAL83
Bank of Montreal InvestorLine	www.investorline.com	1-800-387-7800
Charles Schwab Canada	www.schwabcanada.com	1-888-597-9999
E*Trade Canada	www.canada.etrade.com	1-888-TRADE88
HSBC InvestDirect	www.hsbcinvestdirect.com	1-800-398-1180
CIBC Investor's Edge	www.cibc.com	1-800-567-3343
Sun Life Securities	www.sunsecurities.com	1-800-835-0812
National Bank InvesTel	www.investnet.com	1-800-363-3511
Scotia Discount Brokerage	www.sdbi.com	1-877-536-7493

Executing Your Investment Orders

Tip 76

COMEDIANS ARE FAMOUS FOR NEVER RUSHING TO GET TO A GREAT PUNCH LINE. IN THE RUSH TO FINALLY BUY OR SELL THE STOCK THAT HAS BEEN THE SUBJECT OF SO MUCH RESEARCH AND PLANNING, MANY INVESTORS FORGET ABOUT THE EXECUTION OF THE ORDER. IN OTHER WORDS, THERE IS MORE TO THE GAME THAN SCREAMING "BUY" OR "SELL" AT YOUR BROKER, OR TYPING THE SAME WORDS INTO YOUR INTERNET ORDER FORM. WHETHER YOU USE A FULL-SERVICE OR A DISCOUNT BROKER, IT IS IMPORTANT TO KNOW THE TYPES OF TOOLS THAT YOU HAVE AVAILABLE TO COMPLETE YOUR ORDER AND IN TURN, MAKE MORE MONEY FOR YOURSELF.

Probably the most common orders are market orders to buy or sell a stock. Here, the floor broker on the exchange must execute your order promptly at the most favourable price possible. In reality, what this means is that you will get what you want, but in fast-moving markets, this might happen at a price that is different from the one that you had in mind. Unless otherwise specified, orders are considered to be market orders, which means paying the offer price when buying, or the bid price when selling.

Limit orders are the next category of types of orders. Here the investor imposes a limiting price on the broker, which prevents a broker for paying more for a buy order, or for selling for less for a sell order. An example would be to "buy Sears Canada stock at $60" when Sears Canada stock is trading around the $62 level. This limit order insures that at least the price specified will be obtained. However, the risk is that the order may never get executed. To continue the example, if the market declines during the day to the $60 level, the order will be filled, and the investor will have purchased Sears Canada stock at $60. If the market climbs, the $60 will be surpassed, and the investor will never obtain the stock at that price.

A sell stop order instructs the broker to execute the order when the price falls to, or below, a certain level, at which point it becomes a market order. A stop order may be used to limit a loss or to protect a profit. For example, the buyer of Sears Canada stock at $60, who has now seen the price rise to $70, could protect against an unexpected decline by setting a sell stop order at $66. If the price does decline and the shares do now sell for $66 or less, the paper profit of $6 is protected. A buy stop order is the opposite of a sell stop, and is put into place by an investor who is shorting a stock.

There are numerous order types available, although not every order type is recognized by every discount broker or stockbroker. Contact your firm, or read the fine print in the documents that you obtained when you opened your account.

Investment Clubs—
Exchanging Investment Ideas

Tip 77

INVESTING AND SHARING AREN'T NORMALLY THOUGHT OF AS TWO CONCEPTS

THAT BELONG TOGETHER, BUT THESE ARE THE IDEAS THAT FORM THE BASIS OF

INVESTMENT CLUBS. THE BENEFITS INCLUDE MEETING LIKE-MINDED PEOPLE,

BUT MORE IMPORTANTLY, LEARNING HOW TO INVEST AND APPLY THE DISCIPLINE

NEEDED TO FOLLOW A LONG-TERM APPROACH.

In the United States there are almost 40 000 clubs that are members of the non-profit National Association of Investors Corporation (NAIC), which can be reached at 810-583-6242 or www.better-investing.org. This organization provides various services and advice to the almost three-quarters of a million investors who are members of these local clubs. In Canada, you can contact the Canadian Securities Institute for their book titled *How To Start and Run an Investment Club* at www.investorlearning.ca.

Though clubs take many forms, they are basically groups of 10–20 members, each of whom is expected to attend meetings (typically monthly), make a minimum monthly contribution, and research a particular stock that the club owns or is thinking of purchasing. The members as a whole determine the club's portfolio, with one member dealing with a brokerage to execute the club's orders. The value of each club member's portfolio is determined by the value of all of the club's holdings, apportioned by their initial cash contributions.

You can think of it as a sort of mutual fund, without many of the fees and loads, and requiring more participation from the owners. It also requires a long-term commitment to both the club and its members—you should feel comfortable sharing ideas and participating in a business venture with the other club members.

If you wish to start your own club, the first step, after contacting the organizations above, is to either talk to individuals you know, or approach such ready-made organizations as social clubs, fraternal societies, or other groups to obtain members who wish to participate. You are looking for members who can work well together, share the same long-term investment philosophy (leave the day trading to others), and are willing to put in some effort into researching and selecting some stocks. You will also want a blend of potential members including novices and some who are more familiar with investment methods and approaches.

The first few meetings should be relatively informal and revolve around explaining the purpose and organization of the club. Organization is important, and includes setting out operating procedures, electing officers (including a president to run the meetings, a secretary to maintain minutes, and a treasurer to keep track of dues and investments), setting regular meeting dates, and deciding on the monthly contribution.

Investment clubs can serve as a source for new ideas, a means of keeping you on track during volatile times, and as a sounding board for your own ideas. They are worth your time and effort.

Profiting from the Anomalies—Share Prices Are Not Always Right

Tip 78

INVESTING IN A STOCK IS NEVER EASY. THERE ARE SO MANY DIFFERENT KINDS OF COMPANIES THAT YOU CAN INVEST IN—FAST GROWING COMPANIES, SLOW GROWING COMPANIES, SMALL COMPANIES, BIG COMPANIES, GOOD COMPANIES, AND BAD COMPANIES. EVERY COMPANY HAS ITS OWN UNIQUE RISK AND RETURN CHARACTERISTICS, AND NOT EVERY COMPANY MAKES MONEY FOR ITS INVESTORS.

Over time, investors found indicators that could indicate which companies might outperform the market in the future. These "market anomalies" as they are called (anomalies because they deviate from the idea that all stocks are efficiently priced at all times) have been followed by a range of studies, in attempts to determine the factors that lead to optimal stock performance.

In terms of share prices, anomalies fall into two categories.

VALUE-BASED REGULARITIES

These anomalies suggest that share price returns are associated with several key variables. The theory suggests that companies whose share price is low relative to the amount of money invested into the firm, the sales of the firm, its cash flow, earnings, and dividend yield, make good investments.

- Low price-to-book ratio (P/B). The book value of the firm is equal to the assets of the firm minus the liabilities of the firm; the book value is equal to the amount of money invested by the initial shareholders plus all the reinvested earnings. Low price-to-book ratio (P/B or price of the firm divided by the book value of the firm) companies have outperformed high price-to-book companies.

- Low price-to-sales (P/S). Companies that have a low price-to-sales ratio generate higher rates of return.

- Low price-to-cash flow (P/CF). A company's cash flow is the money they have left in the bank after paying all their bills. Companies that have a low price-to-cash flow ratio generate higher rates of return.

- Low price-to-earnings (P/E). Companies that have a low price-to-earnings ratio generate higher rates of return.

- Dividend yield. The higher the company's dividend yield the higher the rate of return.

EARNINGS EXPECTATION–BASED REGULARITIES

These anomalies suggest that companies who surprise their investors with favourable news (i.e., they improve their expectations for the future) will outperform the market.

- Companies that have been recently upgraded by analysts tend to generate higher investment returns than the stock market.

- Companies that report an earnings surprise tend to outperform going forward.

- Common stocks with high investor expectations tend to underperform the market, and overlooked companies with low investor expectations tend to outperform. This is called the earnings torpedo effect.

- Companies that report earnings late tend to report bad news.

- Companies that are not heavily followed by investors tend to outperform.

Investors should be aware of these historically based market anomalies as they create their diversified investment portfolios.

Profiting from the Anomalies—Stock Markets Are Not Always Right

Tip 79

THERE ARE MANY DIFFERENT FACTORS THAT AFFECT STOCK MARKET LEVELS ON

A MINUTE-TO-MINUTE BASIS. THIS INCLUDES INFLATION DATA, GROSS DOMESTIC

PRODUCT (GDP), INTEREST RATES, UNEMPLOYMENT, SUPPLY, DEMAND, POLITICAL

CHANGES, AND BROADER ECONOMIC FORCES, AMONG OTHERS.

Complicating this are some general market trends, which have been determined historically to exist. Like their share-price-based brothers, these stock market anomalies may provide buying opportunities for investors. These anomalies include:

PRICE-BASED REGULARITIES

- Lower-priced stocks tend to outperform higher-priced stocks, and companies tend to appreciate in value after the announcement of stock split.

- Smaller companies tend to outperform larger companies, which is a key reason for investing in small cap stocks.

- Companies tend to reverse their price direction in the short- and long-term.

- Companies that have a depressed stock price tend to suffer from tax-loss selling in December and bounce back in January.

CALENDAR-BASED REGULARITIES

These regularities allow you to better time your investments in the short-term. Although investors should remember that over the long term the benefits of a regular investment plan (investing each month) far outweigh the benefits of trying to time your investment by a day or two, the following patterns have been shown to occur.

- Time-of-the-day effect. The beginning and the end of the stock market day exhibit different return and volatility characteristics.

- Day-of-the-week effect. The stock markets tend to start the week weak and finish the week strong.

- Week-of-the-month effect. The stock market tends to earn the majority of its returns in the first two weeks of the month.

- Month-of-the-year effect. The first month of the year tends to show increased returns over the rest of the year. This is referred to as the January effect.

Investors should remember that not every anomaly comes about every time, but making sure you're aware of anomalies will allow you to profit over the long-term and deal with market volatility in the short-term. In short, profit from these anomalies, but don't aim to make use of these anomalies at the expense of your long-term investment objectives.

Cheap Stocks Can Make Good Investments

Tip 80

THE KEY TO BECOMING A SUCCESSFUL INVESTOR IS TO KNOW THE DIFFERENCE

BETWEEN A GREAT INVESTMENT AND A BAD INVESTMENT. MANY INVESTORS

ASSUME THAT GREAT COMPANIES ARE GREAT INVESTMENTS, BUT THIS IS NOT

ALWAYS AN ACCURATE ASSESSMENT. SOMETIMES, A WONDERFUL BUSINESS

CAN MAKE A MAKE A LOUSY INVESTMENT. HERE IS WHY.

Most investors can be classified into two investment styles: value and growth. Value investors utilize an investment style that favors good companies at great prices over great companies at good prices. These investors use such valuation measures as price-to-book ratio, price-to-earnings ratio, and dividend yield to determine the attractiveness of an investment. Growth investors invest in companies that are growing their earnings and/or revenue faster than the industry or the overall stock market. These companies usually pay little or no dividends, instead preferring to use profits to finance future expansion and growth. Value investors prefer to own companies at good prices, and growth investors prefer to own great companies and price is a secondary issue.

Which style is better? It depends on the investor. Investors with a lower tolerance for risk should consider investing a larger portion of their portfolio in value stocks. Investors with a higher tolerance for risk should consider investing a larger portion of their portfolio in growth stocks. However, investors who want to avoid underperforming the stock market as whole should always invest at least a small portion of their portfolio in both investment styles.

Over the long term, value has outperformed growth, but from time to time growth has outperformed during the short term. During 1999, for example, growth stocks outperformed value stocks by 40 per cent.

INDEX	RATE OF RETURN
BARRA Growth	9.7%
BARRA Value	12.5%
TSE 300	11.4%

Annualized rate of return from 1982 to 2000

Investors should be aware of the following.

- The stock market rewards different styles at different times.

- Value investors tend to be buy-and-hold investors, and growth investors tend to be more short-term oriented.

- It is very difficult to determine which style will outperform in the short-term.

- The variance between performance of value and growth styles can be very large during short time frames.

- For some growth stocks, growth never does come. Eventually the share price falls.

- Some value stocks are cheap for a reason—they are bad stocks and they deserve to be cheap.

Overall, the best investments are those companies that are able to grow profits and add shareholder value. These companies have traditionally been value companies. Investors who prefer to select their own stocks should consider a value approach and complement these investments with a growth mutual fund. Remember that selecting the wrong growth company is not as forgiving as selecting a value company erroneously, as the market correction in growth stocks in early 2000 showed us.

The Trend Is Your Friend

Tip 81

MOMENTUM STRATEGIES ARE THE RODNEY DANGERFIELD OF THE INVESTMENT WORLD: THEY DON'T GET ANY RESPECT. COMPARED TO THE WORK THAT IS NECESSARY FOR FUNDAMENTAL ANALYSIS, THE MOMENTUM STRATEGIES OF TECHNICAL ANALYSIS SEEM ALMOST TOO SIMPLE. HERE, YOU ARE NOT STUDYING ANY NUMBERS OR ASSESSING A COMPANY'S PROSPECTS. RATHER, YOU ARE BUYING BECAUSE THE STOCK IS GOING UP. PUT ANOTHER WAY, INSTEAD OF THE CLASSIC "BUY LOW, SELL HIGH," WITH MOMENTUM STRATEGIES YOU "BUY HIGH, AND SELL HIGHER." AND UNLIKE SOME OTHER STRATEGIES, THIS ONE COMES WITH DEFINITE SELL SIGNALS: YOU SELL A STOCK WHEN IT STOPS PERFORMING.

Studies first reported in academic journals in the 1960s showed that purchasing stocks that were leaders in relative price performance in the previous 26 weeks would yield above-market performance, albeit with much higher portfolio risk. Later studies added some further caveats: that there were periods of time, especially in the 1930s and 1940s, that relative strength strategies underperformed a simple buy and hold approach. Still more research led to the general conclusion that relative strength strategies perform best during periods of rising markets, while during and immediately after times of market weakness such a strategy will underperform.

Most recently, James O'Shaughnessy showed how various strategies would have performed over a 45-year period in his book *What Works On Wall Street*. A strategy of creating a portfolio of the 50 stocks that showed the best one-year price appreciation from the previous year would have outperformed the market, but with a high risk attached (there were some years when the portfolio dropped by 20 per cent or more). Conversely, the 50 stocks with the worst one-year price performance showed a compound growth rate of around 3 per cent, far below the general market's compound annual return during this time of over 13 per cent. In Canada, Steve Foerster from the Richard Ivey School of Business at the University of Western Ontario has shown that these persistencies are found in Canadian stock markets as well.

Clearly there is something worth noticing here, but there are cautions as well. The high volatility and sometimes prolonged periods that any momentum strategy has underperformed the market can tax the nerves of even the most diehard momentum investor. Secondly, such an investor has to resign himself to the fact that he will never be getting in on the ground floor of any stock or portfolio movement, as momentum strategies only allow you to buy once a trend has been established. Investors who want to invest in a mutual fund that applies this strategy could consider the AIM Canada Growth Fund or the Synergy Canadian Growth or Momentum Class.

Going Against the Tide

Tip 82

TRADITIONALLY, INVESTORS HAVE BEEN TOLD TO INVEST FOR THE LONG-TERM—
BUY LOW AND SELL HIGH, AND DIVERSIFY. THOSE WHO HAVE ADHERED TO THESE
PRINCIPALS HAVE BECOME VERY SUCCESSFUL. HOWEVER, THERE ARE SOME
INVESTORS WHO DO NOT GO THIS ROUTE, BUT INSTEAD AIM TO EARN A HIGH
RATE OF RETURN WHEN THE MARKET DECLINES. THESE INVESTORS "SHORT" A
STOCK: INSTEAD OF PURCHASING SHARES OF A COMPANY THEY THINK IS GOING
TO APPRECIATE THEY BORROW SHARES OF A COMPANY THEY THINK IS GOING TO
DECLINE IN VALUE AND SELL THEM. AFTER THE SHARES HAVE DECLINED IN VALUE
THEY REPURCHASE THE SHARES AT A LOWER PRICE AND GIVE THEM BACK TO THE
ORIGINAL LENDER.

Let's illustrate the concept. Suppose you think that shares of BCE are overvalued and will
drop from the current price of $180. You call your broker and tell him that you want to
sell short 200 shares of BCE. In order to short a stock you will have to establish a margin
account that has the ability to short stocks. Your broker then borrows (on your behalf) 200
shares of BCE and sells them for you, depositing $36 000 in your margin account. Now

you need the price of BCE shares to decline in value because eventually you will need to return the 200 borrowed shares to your broker. If the shares of BCE decline in value by $20, you can then buy 200 shares of BCE at $160 for a total cost of $32 000 and pocket the $4000 difference ($36 000 minus $32 000), minus any commissions incurred.

Investors should realize that shorting shares of a company is a lot riskier than buying shares because the price of the shares could rise by an unlimited amount. In turn, the investor could incur unlimited losses. For example, if the share price of BCE goes up by $60, you would have to pay $48 000 to buy the 200 shares owed to your broker. In this scenario, you would lose $12 000 ($36 000–$48 000) plus the commission.

Since shorting stocks involves a lot more risk, securities commissions have implemented special regulations requiring brokers to issue a margin call, meaning that investors have to deposit additional funds with their broker when their losses reach a certain amount, in order to cover the decline from the investment. Another risk comes from the original lender of the shorter security, who may ask that the security be returned, and if no other lender can be found the investor will be forced to return the stock at the current market price. Thus, short selling is an excellent way to make money but investors should be aware of the unique risk and return characteristics associated with this approach.

A Time to Sell

Tip 83

NOTHING LASTS FOREVER, AND THE OFTEN FORGOTTEN FLIP SIDE OF EVERY INVESTMENT IS KNOWING WHEN TO SELL. NOT EVERY COMPANY MAINTAINS GOOD GROWTH POTENTIAL, GREAT MANAGEMENT, AND SELLS AT LESS THAN ITS INTRINSIC VALUE. INVESTORS NEED TO BE ABLE TO PROTECT THEIR GAINS WHEN A FORMERLY GREAT INVESTMENT IS PAST ITS PRIME.

Of course there are some valid reasons not to sell in a great hurry. Strip bonds, for example, are great if you hold them to maturity. Some investments are also hard to sell early—many mutual funds, for example, are subject to early redemption fees if you sell within a stated period.

There is one simple rule for knowing when to sell—if the reason for buying the stock in the first place is gone, then sell. Many investors still continue to hold their stock thinking their short-term investment is suddenly a long-term investment to be held through thick and thin.

Here are some guidelines to help you set your own selling parameters and determine when things change:

Sell when something fundamental changes. Change comes in many forms. Perhaps some key economic fundamentals have changed over time, affecting a sector or country mutual fund. Maybe a hot money manager has left a fund. A mutual fund can change over time, though the manager and stated goals remain the same. This is called style drift; some managers have been known to adapt their investment approach, often in an attempt to chase returns. Funds that are supposed to be broadly diversified may end up being heavily weighted in a sector or geographic area that runs contrary to your investment outlook. All of these are warning flags, and should be considered in your decision to sell or keep holding. On the personal side, your own life changes and need for cash flow will affect your overall risk tolerance, and thus the types of investments you hold.

Sell to rebalance your portfolio. Rebalancing may occur because of the superior performance of a sector, which has effectively unbalanced your overall portfolio. A long bull market in stocks will change the mix between bonds and stocks in your portfolio, requiring some rebalancing.

Sell when something better comes along. One way of looking at any investment is that you should think about selling an investment the minute you have decided to make that purchase. In other words, don't fall in love with a stock, mutual fund, or other investment. Constantly scan the investment horizon for any investment that will better suit your needs. The investment field is always changing and offering new products. You should consider new investment alternatives; each month the mutual fund industry introduces an average of 30 new funds—some may fit your needs better.

Always think about selling, but remember that stock markets have a reputation for overreacting to good and bad news—don't pay too much for an investment and don't sell for too little.

Nine

The Tax Man

This chapter deals with taxes and your investment. If you look at your pay stub you will notice that tax is likely your largest bill each year. Most taxpayers easily pay more than $10 000 of tax in a year, so saving an extra 10 per cent will put an additional $1000 into your pocket. The following is a roundup of some tax tips as they affect your investments. Apply them and save money.

The concepts of tax planning, investment planning, and financial planning are frequently used interchangeably during the investment management process. However, they are not synonymous. Tax planning is an effective tool to increase your after-tax returns by reducing taxes payable. Investment planning helps you maximize your investment returns, and financial planning allows you to effectively manage your financial affairs.

Income splitting is a tax planning strategy in which an investor aims to reduce the overall taxes paid by the family. The taxpayer attempts to transfer a portion of income to a family member in a lower tax bracket. In recent years the CCRA has limited the ability of Canadian taxpayers to split income but there are still several strategies that investors could and should consider to reduce their family's overall tax bill each April. The Agency has the ability to limit income splitting through the use of "attribution" rules. Therefore, the key to effective income splitting is to track your investments and expenditures, and to plan ahead.

This chapter will introduce several ways that you can shift income from a higher-income earner to a lower-income earner. To effectively utilize an income splitting strategy to reduce your taxes you have to know what your marginal tax rate is. Your marginal tax rate is the tax rate that applies to your next dollar earned. The table below shows the marginal tax rates. With the Canadian tax system, you do not pay the highest tax rate on all of your income, only on the income that falls within a particular tax bracket. For example, if you earn $35 000 per year you will have to pay 26 per cent tax on the first $30 004 and 40 per cent on the remainder.

Marginal tax rates and income splitting is based on a progressive tax system. The more money you earn the more you get taxed. Thus, it is important for high-income earners who pay lots of tax to split their income with family members who earn less and don't pay lots of tax.

TAXABLE INCOME BRACKETS	FEDERAL TAX RATE	COMBINED FEDERAL AND PROVINCIAL TAX RATE *
$30 004 or less	17%	26%
Between $34 005 and $60 009	26%	40%
$60 010 and over	29%	45%

Assumes a surtax of 3 per cent and a provincial tax rate of 50 per cent. Actual figures will vary depending on the province you live in.

Let's illustrate the concept of income splitting using an example. Jack and his spouse Jill want to reduce their tax bill. Jack earns $75 000 per year and Jill, who works part-time, makes $24 000 per year. If Jack earns an additional $1000 per year from his investments he will have to pay $450 in taxes and he gets to keep the rest. However, if Jill earned $1000 in interest per year from her investments she would have to pay 26 per cent or $260 in tax, $190 less than Jack. Therefore, it would be more advantageous for Jill to earn an extra dollar than Jack. Thus, Jack and Jill should attempt to arrange their financial affairs to maximize their after-tax income. The following tips will illustrate how investors can structure their financial affairs to maximize their after-tax income.

Before we get started here are a few points that should provide a good frame of reference, and which will allow you to easily comprehend some of the tax tips.

- Remember that income can be split through the use of a spousal RRSP.

- Remember that attribution rules prohibit investors from splitting income with family members after it's earned—you have to structure income splitting beforehand. For example, an investor lends money to a spouse for the purpose of earning business income (business income is not attributable), and through a salary paid to a spouse for services performed in a business owned by an investor.

- Also remember that while money transferred to a spouse for investments is attributed back to the investor, the income that is earned on the reinvested capital, in other words the income on the income, is not attributed back and is taxed in the hands of the spouse.

- Income can be split with children. Money can be gifted to children 18 years old and over without any income attribution (perhaps to contribute to their own RRSP and thus reduce their income) there is attribution if the child is under the age of 18.

- Dividend income should be generated in the hands of the higher income-earning spouse, who can thus make use of the dividend tax credit, which can only be used if there is taxable income.

- Remember that when an asset is sold at a loss and reacquired by either you or a related party within a period beginning 30 days prior to the sale or 30 days after the date of the sale, the loss is not deductible. Why is this important? A transfer of an asset into an RRSP is actually counted as a deemed disposition, which will generate either a capital gain or a capital loss. If there is a capital loss it will be denied, for the reasons above, as a superficial loss. Thus, you have to either sell the asset, for a capital loss, or use the cash to make a contribution and the purchase of a different asset within your RRSP, or you can wait a period longer than the 30 days to reacquire the property within your RRSP.

- Investors gravitate to some complex tax shelters to defer taxes to some point in the future. Don't neglect the obvious—an RRSP allows for deferral as well as compound, tax-sheltered growth. Until you have used up all of your contribution room, don't go chasing after exotic tax shelters if the underlying investment is without merit—there is no sense paying a dollar to save fifty cents in tax.

- In a similar fashion, make use of RESPs if they are applicable, and if you are at the top marginal rate and have used up your RRSP contributions, look at universal life products.

- Why wait for a big refund cheque in April? If you have made a large contribution to your RRSP early in the year, or if you have participated in a tax shelter, you should apply to the Canada Customs and Revenue Agency for permission to reduce your withholding taxes at source on income, such as income from employment.

Remember that a little tax planning ahead can save you a lot of money in April.

We know that taxpayers who make more money have to pay tax at a higher tax rate than taxpayers that make less money. It is also important to remember that income earned from different sources is also taxed differently. To encourage risk taking and have a fair tax system you have to pay less tax on certain investments. Our first tip will highlight the difference between different sources of income while the following table discloses what types of income are derived from different investments. Interest is taxed at the highest rates and dividends (income received from a corporation) and capital gains (when you sell an investment at a higher price than your cost) are taxed at a lower rate.

TYPE OF INVESTMENT	TYPE OF INCOME
Guaranteed Investment Certificates (GIC's)	Interest
Canada Savings Bonds	Interest
Bonds (of all types)	Interest, capital gains
Money Market Mutual Funds	Interest
Bond Funds, Mortgage Funds	Interest, capital gains
Bonds of all types	Interest, capital gains
Balanced Funds	Interest, dividends, capital gains
Real Estate	Interest, dividends, capital gains
Dividend-Paying Stocks	Dividends, capital gains
Common Shares	Dividends, capital gains
Equity Mutual Funds	Dividends, capital gains

In addition to highlighting the different tax rates from different investments we cover taxes and your mutual funds, how to split income among your family, and how to make charitable contributions using your investments. We will also show you how you can save taxes by moonlighting, how to defer taxes with sector funds, how to claim your foreign tax credits, and what to do if you disagree with the taxman. Please note that taxpayers with complex tax situations should consult their accountant or other tax professional.

Interest Income, Dividends, and Capital Gains—Is There a Difference?

Tip 84

MANY INVESTORS ASSUME THAT INTEREST INCOME, DIVIDEND INCOME, AND CAPITAL GAINS ARE ALL TAXED IN THE SAME MANNER. HOWEVER, THIS IS NOT THE CASE, AND INVESTORS SHOULD PAY ATTENTION TO THE SECURITIES THAT PROVIDE A HIGHER AFTER-TAX RATE OF RETURN. NOT EVERY INVESTMENT IS CREATED EQUAL FROM A TAX PERSPECTIVE, AND KNOWING THE DIFFERENCE CAN MAKE AND SAVE YOU MONEY.

Interest income earned from bonds is fully taxable at your marginal rate. Dividend income earned by investing in preferred shares and common stocks is taxed at a lower rate (taxpayers receive a dividend tax credit), while two-thirds of your capital gains are fully taxable. The following table highlights the different after-tax rates of return for the three different sources of income. It compares the after-tax return of an investment that generated a pretax return of 10 per cent. An investor who is in the lowest tax bracket and invested in a fixed income investment would earn an after-tax rate of return of 7.37 per cent. However, if that same investor invested in a stock that earned a pre-tax return of 10 per cent, then their after-tax rate of return would have been 8.25 per cent.

AFTER-TAX YIELD ON A 10 PER CENT INVESTMENT

TAXABLE INCOME BRACKETS	TAX RATE*	INTEREST	DIVIDEND	CAPITAL GAIN
$30 004 or less	26%	7.37%	9.2%	8.25%
Between $30 005 and $60 009	40%	5.98%	7.5%	7.32%
$60 010 and over	45%	5.52%	6.9%	7.01%

Assumes a surtax of 3 per cent and a provincial tax rate of 50 per cent.

The following table highlights the break-even rate of return. For example, as shown above, a taxpayer in the highest tax bracket would earn a 5.52 per cent after tax return by investing in a Guaranteed Income Certificate (GIC) that yielded 10 per cent before tax. The following table illustrates that the same investor would need to earn an 8 per cent dividend yield or a 7.87 per cent capital gain to earn the same after tax return of 5.52 per cent.

BREAK-EVEN RATE OF RETURN ON A 10 PER CENT INVESTMENT

TAXABLE INCOME BRACKETS	TAX RATE*	INTEREST	DIVIDEND	CAPITAL GAIN
$30 004 or less	26%	10.00%	8.00%	8.94%
Between $30 005 and $60 009	40%	10.00%	8.00%	8.17%
$60 010 and over	45%	10.00%	8.00%	7.87%

Assumes a surtax of 3 per cent and a provincial tax rate of 50 per cent.

There are some clear winners in the after-tax investment comparison. Over the long run, higher rates of return and better tax treatment make preferred shares and common stocks a very prudent component of a diversified investment portfolio.

Taxes and Your Mutual Funds

Tip 85

THERE ARE MANY GOOD REASONS FOR INVESTING IN MUTUAL FUNDS, BUT ONE ADVANTAGE IS THE SIMPLICITY OF TAX REPORTING—SOMEBODY ELSE MAKES THE INVESTMENT DECISIONS AND DOES THE PAPERWORK. BUT NO MATTER HOW MUCH OF THIS WORK IS DELEGATED TO THE FUND MANAGERS, THERE IS STILL SOME RECORD KEEPING THAT IS VERY NECESSARY WHEN IT COMES TO TAXATION MATTERS.

Mutual funds can be thought of, for taxation purposes, as a shell. This shell receives dividends and income from the investments that it holds, and can incur capital gains or losses from the securities it trades during the year. This shell, in turn, pays no income taxes—dividends, interest, and capital gains that it makes are passed on to you, the investor. The income that is paid out retains the same form as what it was within the mutual fund—interest is paid out as interest, capital gains as capital gains, and dividends as dividends. All of this is made clear on the information slip, which the mutual fund company sends out to investors at tax time. Investors pay tax at different rates, depending on the types of income received (interest income at the full marginal rate, capital gains at 2/3 the rate, and dividends are grossed up and subject to the dividend tax credit.) Depending on the type of investments held within the fund, there might be little or even no income in some of these three classes.

This is fairly straightforward, but there is more. Many people never receive these distributions, as they choose to reinvest this money in additional mutual fund units. However, even though you may not have received a cheque in the mail from the income distribution, the entire process is treated for tax purposes as if you had received this money and then gone out and made a purchase of new units.

What this means is that to avoid double taxation this process must be tracked—the amount that has been distributed, reported and taxed, is added back to the original purchase price to form a new adjusted cost base. Here is an example. Assume that in 1997 you invested $10 000 in a fund with a 4 per cent front-end load and a selling price of $10 per share throughout the period of the example. Distributions were reinvested in 1998 and 1999, and in that year an additional purchase of shares was made. The adjusted cost base calculation is shown below:

TRACKING YOUR COST BASE

TRANSACTION	AMOUNT	OF SHARES
Initial Purchase, 1997	$ 9 600	960
Load on Initial Purchase, 1997	400	-
Reinvestment, 1998	300	27
Reinvestment, 1999	400	33
Purchase, 1999	960	74
Load on Purchase, 1999	40	-
TOTAL	$ 11 700	1 094

In total you have 1094 units at an adjusted cost base of ($11 700/1094=$10.69) $10.69 per share. If you were to sell shares today at a price of $12.00, your capital gain per share would be ($12.00–$10.69) $1.31 per share and not just the simple current price ($12.00) minus the starting price ($10.00). Keeping the paperwork up-to-date saves you taxes, as this example shows.

All in the Family—You Pay the Bills While I Make the Investments

Tip 86

YOUR MARRIAGE IS LIKELY ONE OF THE BIGGEST DECISIONS IN YOUR LIFE, BUT AFTER THE WEDDING YOU ALSO HAVE ANOTHER BIG DECISION—WHETHER OR NOT TO POOL YOUR FINANCES, AND GENERALLY HOW TO ARRANGE YOUR FINANCIAL AFFAIRS. IF YOU AND YOUR SPOUSE HAVE DIFFERENT MARGINAL TAX RATES, HOW YOU STRUCTURE YOUR INVESTMENTS WILL BE VERY IMPORTANT. YOU WANT TO ENSURE THAT THE PERSON MAKING THE LEAST MONEY IS MAKING THE BULK OF THE INVESTMENTS, WHICH WILL ENSURE THAT BOTH OF YOU PAY THE LEAST TAX ON YOUR INVESTMENTS.

The Canada Customs and Revenue Agency keeps a very close eye on taxpayers, their spouses, and their children when they transfer property or investments to each other. The Tax Act has rules that are intended to prevent taxpayers from transferring investments to spouses or children, commonly referred to as the attribution rules. These rules transfer any tax liability back to the original owner for tax purposes. For example, Jack gave his wife $10 000 to invest in a Guaranteed Income Certificate (GIC) because she was at a lower tax rate. Jack thought any income earned would be taxable in the hands of Jill. However, the

Canada Customs and Revenue Agency will attribute back the income earned on the GIC to Jack, who will then pay the tax based on his marginal rate

Jill can make the investment and she can receive the income, but if Jack gave her the initial money to make the investment, Jack will pay the tax. Thus, it is important to prove to the CCRA that Jill made the investment. The CCRA will ask Jill to trace the source of funds that allowed her to make this investment. Sources of funds means the total of Jill's income, less any expenses she paid. If Jill earned $24 000 in a year and after paying for the mortgage and the car is left with $1000, but in the same year made a $20 000 investment and earned $1000 interest, the Canada Customs and Revenue Agency will attribute that interest income back to Jack. It would argue that after Jill's expense are taken into account she did not have $20 000 to invest and thus the money must have come from Jack.

The solution is to have the higher income earner pay all the joint bills. This includes the mortgage, the car, the groceries—everything that the higher income earner can afford. Then, the lower income spouse sets up a second bank account, with all of her paycheques directly deposited into this account. This is the account used as the source for investment funds. Any income earned on this investment will be taxed in the hands of Jill. Jack and Jill have a perfect "paper trail" to show that the investment was funded from money earned by Jill because it came from her bank account. Having separate bank accounts and a good paper trail can increase your after tax returns if, like Jack and Jill, you and your spouse have different marginal tax rates.

Making Interest Payments Tax Deductible

Tip 87

BORROWED MONEY HAS ALLOWED YOU TO PURCHASE MANY BIG-TICKET ITEMS SUCH AS YOUR CAR, COTTAGE, HOME, AND MAYBE EVEN MAKE YOUR RRSP CONTRIBUTIONS. INTEREST PAID ON PERSONAL CONSUMPTION SUCH AS CREDIT CARDS, CONSUMER LOANS, AND MORTGAGES IS NOT TAX DEDUCTIBLE, WHILE INTEREST PAID ON LOANS FOR PURCHASES IN INCOME-GENERATING INVESTMENTS LIKE STOCKS, REAL PROPERTY, AND BUSINESSES CAN BE DEDUCTED. IN ADDITION, SHORT-TERM INTEREST CHARGES ON CONSUMER LOANS SUCH AS CREDIT CARDS ARE HIGHER THAN INTEREST CHARGES ON LOANS MADE FOR INVESTMENT PURPOSES. INVESTORS WHO NEED TO BORROW MONEY TO FINANCE A PURCHASE SHOULD FIRST BORROW MONEY FOR THEIR INVESTMENTS AND OTHER INCOME-PRODUCING ASSETS, AND THEN BORROW MONEY TO FINANCE THEIR CONSUMER SPENDING.

In general, loans made to earn ordinary income from a business, investments, or property are tax deductible. The income can come from interest, dividends, rents, or the profits from a business. It does not include the earnings from capital gains, or of capital gains dividends from mutual funds. All of this is highly advantageous because investors are able to reduce their tax bill while (in theory) their investment appreciates in value and provides income along the way. Of course this approach only makes sense if, over the long-term, the investment generates a rate of return greater than the interest rate charged on the loan, on an after-tax basis.

If you invest in an investment that does not have the potential to generate a sufficiently high rate of return, then the interest may not be tax deductible. The Canada Customs and Revenue Agency holds that investors must have a reasonable assurance that they will be able to earn a profit otherwise the deduction may not be allowed. For example, an investor who borrows money at 15 per cent to invest in a fixed income investment that yields 5 per cent will not have a reasonable assurance of making a profit. In this example, the investor will only be able to deduct the first 5 per cent of their interest expenses because the interest deduction will be equal to the return on the fixed income investment. In contrast, an investor who borrows money at 15 per cent and invests in an investment that has the potential to earn a higher rate of return will be able to deduct the entire interest expense when incurred.

Investors should structure their loans to ensure that interest expenses are tax deductible wherever possible. For example, if you have a mortgage or a credit card balance as well as investments outside your RRSP, you should sell these investments and use the proceeds to reduce or eliminate your outstanding debt. You can then borrow new funds to repurchase your investments. This strategy will allow you to deduct interest expenses. It is important to note that you are not increasing your debt load—you are just configuring your debt in a manner that allows you to deduct your interest expenses. In turn, you are improving your net worth.

Honey! Can You Lend Me $20?

Tip 88

LENDING MONEY WITHIN A FAMILY, EITHER TO A SPOUSE OR TO A CHILD, GOES ON ALL THE TIME. HOWEVER, IT IS POSSIBLE TO SAVE ON TAXES IF YOU LOAN YOUR SPOUSE OR MINOR CHILD MONEY TO INVEST.

As was mentioned earlier, the Canada Customs and Revenue Agency has a set of attribution rules that transfer any tax liability back to the original owner for tax purposes. For example Jack, who is a high-income earner, gave his wife Jill, who earns less and is at a lower marginal tax rate, $10 000 to buy 100 shares in Nortel Networks. The following year Jill sold the shares and realized a gain of $5000. Jack thought that Jill would have to pay tax on this amount. However, the CCRA will attribute back the capital gains earned on Nortel Networks back to Jack and the gain will be taxed in his hands.

Attribution affects income, dividends, rent, and capital gains earned on investments made by the lower income-earning spouse, but financed by the higher income earner. Attribution affects income, dividends, rent, but not capital gains earned on investments made by minor children but financed by the higher income parent.

Taxpayers should realize that there are two options to consider in order to effectively split income over the long term.

- Attribution does not apply on reinvested income. Said differently, if the high-income earning spouse finances the investment for a lower income-earning spouse they will have to pay taxes on the income earned. However, if the lower income earner reinvests that money, subsequent income is taxable in the hands of the lower income earner. For example, Jack invests $1000 in Jill's name in a one-year Guaranteed Income Certificate (GIC) that yields 5 per cent. In a year Jack will have to pay taxes on the $50, but Jill can invest this money and any interest earned on the $50 will be taxable in Jill's hands. Over time this can add up.

- You can also avoid attribution rules by lending money to your spouse or minor child at the prescribed rate of interest. The prescribed rate of interest is the minimum interest expense that you must charge your spouse or minor child for borrowing the money to invest. The interest payment must also be made to the higher income earner within 30 days of December 31. Therefore, a higher income earner can finance an investment for a lower income earner and receive a prescribed rate of interest each year from that lower income spouse. The lower income earner can invest in stocks and bonds and potentially earn a higher rate of return than the prescribed rate being paid, and pay tax on the difference at a lower tax rate.

Taking the Allowance to the Next Step

Tip 89

ONE OF THE MOST EFFECTIVE WAYS THAT A FAMILY CAN STRUCTURE ITS INVEST-MENT FINANCES IS TO LET YOUR CHILDREN INVEST MONEY IN GROWTH INVEST-MENTS THAT EARN CAPITAL GAINS. NOT ONLY ARE CAPITAL GAINS TAXED AT A LOWER TAX RATE, AS WE HAVE SEEN, BUT CAPITAL GAINS EARNED BY MINOR CHILDREN ARE TAXABLE IN THEIR HANDS.

Here are some definitions. A capital gain is the amount by which the proceeds of a sale exceed the cost associated with the acquisition and disposition of that capital property. For investment purposes, this includes stock in a company, investments, mutual funds, real estate, art, antiques, cars, a cottage, and other personal property.

Once you dispose of such an asset at a gain you have to pay tax on that gain. Since the Canada Customs and Revenue Agency wants to encourage investors to take risks, and investing in capital assets usually entails some risk, as an incentive only 66.6 per cent of your gain (which was recently lowered from 75 per cent) are taxed at your marginal rate. You are also allowed to reduce your realized capital gains with any capital losses you may have. However capital gains are also unique because of the attribution rules relating to minor children.

Let's consider Jack and Jill and their 13-year-old daughter, Jean. Jack has an extra $10 000 for investment purposes. If Jack earns an additional $1000 per year from his investments in capital gains he will have to pay $340 in tax because he is in the higher tax bracket. Because Jack and Jill are husband and wife, he can't give the money to Jill, because the tax would be attributed back to him.

However, taxpayers can shift capital property to their minor children, defined as a child under 18 years of age. Any capital gain earned on those investments will not be taxed in the hands of the original donor. In the example above, if Jean invested the money, any capital gains earned on the investment would be taxable in her hands. If Jean has no other source of income, it would be an effective way for the family to reduce their entire tax bill.

Once Jean has made the investment it would be a good idea for her to realize a capital gain periodically. Taxes are not payable on capital gains until they are realized. All investors, including Jean, should think ahead about when to sell their investment, because they will want to avoid selling in a year when there is much taxable income. Thus, in years when Jean has no other income she should sell the investment and trigger (crystalize) the capital gain.

Don't Forget the Little Things

Tip 90

MANY CONSUMERS SPEND AN HOUR PER MONTH CLIPPING COUPONS OR SHOPPING AT THREE DIFFERENT STORES IN ORDER TO SAVE $20. SAVING $20 FOR AN HOUR OF WORK IS A GOOD RETURN FOR THE AMOUNT OF TIME SPENT. HOWEVER, OFTEN THE SAME PERSON WILL SKIP THROUGH THEIR TAXES TO GET THE WHOLE ORDEAL OVER WITH AS QUICKLY AS POSSIBLE. AS A RESULT THESE INVESTORS PAY HUNDREDS OR EVEN THOUSANDS OF DOLLARS MORE IN INCOME TAX EACH YEAR.

The reason investors don't deduct some of the costs associated with investments is a function of both the size of some of these deductions (many are seemingly minor), and lack of knowledge of the full range of available deductions. Investors who earn income from their investments are allowed to deduct the following common deductions.

- Interest expenses. Any interest paid on a loan made for investment purposes can be deducted from income, investment, or employment income.

- Carrying charges. These charges are tax deductible if they were incurred to earn investment income. Examples of carrying charges include fees paid for a safety deposit box, Canada Savings Bonds payroll deduction fees, insurance policy loan interest, and custody fees. Remember that RRSP administration fees are no longer deductible—the same goes for RRIF fees.

- Investment counselling fees. Investors who pay investment-counselling fees outside of their investments can receive a tax deduction equal to the amount of the investment counselling fees incurred and paid. Paying investment-counselling fees directly is very common with pooled funds. Unfortunately, for mutual fund investors the mutual fund pays the investment counselling fees directly to the management company on behalf of the fund. Thus, investors who invest in mutual funds will not be able to claim a deduction for the mutual fund's fees, though they will be able to deduct any fees associated with the investment advisor who recommended the fund's purchase.

- Legal and accounting fees. These fees must be incurred for the purpose of earning income. Legal fees incurred to buy a home will not be tax deductible but legal fees incurred to conduct an appeal of taxes can be deducted.

- Foreign non-business income tax credit. Investors who invest outside of Canada are generally subject to foreign withholding tax in that country. Investors are able to claim a tax credit for the withholding taxes incurred, although some limitations apply. If you received a dividend from a foreign corporation make sure you know what the withholding taxes were.

Thus, investors have the ability to deduct certain costs associated with earning income. While not all of these costs are applicable to every investor, make sure that you make full use of what is relevant to you. Consult your accountant for any other deductions that may apply to any of your own investments.

Using Your Investments for Charity

Tip 91

IF YOU ARE THE AVERAGE CANADIAN, AFTER PAYING THE BILLS AND INVESTING A SMALL PORTION OF YOUR INCOME THERE IS USUALLY VERY LITTLE LEFT OVER TO DONATE FOR CHARITY. THERE IS SOMETHING YOU CAN DO THAT WILL HELP BOTH YOURSELF AND THE CHARITY YOU DONATE TO.

A charitable donation will allow you to claim a two-tiered tax credit. The first $200 of your donation will provide you with a 17 per cent tax credit, which comes out to a $34 federal tax credit. After taking into consideration the provincial tax rate, this will be about 27 per cent overall, or $54. Any money that you donate in excess of $200 within the tax year will entitle you to a 29 per cent tax credit and after taking into consideration the provincial tax rate this will total about 50 per cent.

Donations can be transferred and grouped between spouses. Thus, it makes sense for one spouse to claim the combined donations of both spouses, in order to get above the $200 floor. As credits can be carried forward for a period of up to five years, it is prudent for taxpayers to defer claiming any deductions in one year if they are below the $200 thresh-old. You can carry forward these deductions to the next year and claim the tax credit when your donations are above the $200 minimum.

There is an upper limit for charitable deductions, which is 75 per cent of a taxpayer's net income. Any portion above this ceiling can be carried forward for up to five years. In the year of death and the year immediately preceding death this limit rises to 100 per cent.

To claim a charitable donation, you must have an official receipt that shows the organization's charitable registration number. This means that it is worthwhile to track down the official receipts that you will receive from various pledges and small gifts.

Here is the real kicker. You can also donate property or investments to a charity as an alternative to donating money or to selling the investment and then donating the proceeds. Thus, taxpayers who want to claim a charitable donation but do not have the money to give could gift their investments and claim the tax credit.

Individuals who donate investments or mutual funds only have to include in their taxable income 37.5 per cent of the capital gain resulting from the deemed disposition. This is instead of the usual 66.6 per cent for capital gains. This only applies to donations in kind made between February 18, 1997 and the end of 2001. At the end of 2001 Ottawa will review this measure in order to determine its effectiveness in stimulating higher donations. It is clearly better for you to donate investments than cash because you have a lower tax liability and a higher charitable donation tax credit. There are other advantages to this strategy including higher capital gains ceilings, and you should discuss it with your tax advisor if this appeals to you.

Moonlighting

Tip 92

FOR MANY ENTREPRENEURS SELF-EMPLOYMENT IS THE ULTIMATE DREAM. IN ADDITION TO THE FREEDOM AND POTENTIAL REWARDS, PEOPLE WHO ARE SELF-EMPLOYED HAVE MORE FLEXIBILITY IN THEIR TAX PLANNING THAN THOSE WHO ARE EMPLOYED BY OTHERS.

There are many misconceptions around being self-employed. You don't have to be incorporated, and you don't have to hire other people, and you do not need to do it on a full-time basis. The Canada Customs and Revenue Agency considers a business to be any activity that is conducted for a profit, or a reasonable expectation of a profit. The last point is very important as many self-employed people work long hours and some may never make any money. Being self-employed isn't easy and thus one option you may want to consider is being self-employed as a second job.

Do you have a hobby that you could turn into a business? Do you have an idea that you would like to pursue that could turn into a profitable opportunity? Having a second self-employed business won't necessarily make you millions of dollars, but it can add to your income and to your cash flow.

Generally speaking, self-employed individuals may deduct from their self-employment income all of the expenses that are related to their business, are reasonable under the circumstances, and are not otherwise limited. This includes:

- Capital assets. The capital cost allowance (CCA) allows the self-employed to deduct the cost of capital assets such as office furniture and computers. This is subject to certain rules and schedules that can be found at the Canada Customs and Revenue Agency's web site www.ccra-adrc.gc.ca.

- Accounting, legal, and related professional service fees.

- Transportation expenses, with limitations on the vehicle itself.

- The cost of supplies and materials.

- Meals and entertainment (deductible at a rate of 50 per cent).

- Office expenses (postage, stationary, telephone, etc.).

- Bank charges.

- Insurance premiums.

- Convention and meeting expenses, with certain limitations.

- Bad debts.

- Housing expenses, when the office is in the home. These expenses are limited to the self-employment business income that exists before the deductions are taken. In other words, an office in the home cannot be used to create a business loss.

- Memberships and periodical subscriptions related to the business.

- Salaries paid to family members, including a spouse or children. This salary may then allow the family member to become eligible to make an RRSP contribution based on this earned income.

Keeping up with the bookkeeping involved with income taxes and the GST can be time consuming. You will need to keep accurate records and get professional tax and accounting help, sometimes even before you consider starting a business. However, having a business provides excellent strategies to split income among family members, can be useful for estate planning purposes, has tax advantages, and can make you money.

Your U.S. Investments

Tip 93

WITH MORE AND MORE CANADIANS INVESTING IN U.S.-BASED INVESTMENTS FOR HIGHER RETURNS AND DIVERSIFICATION, THERE ARE SOME PARTICULAR TAXATION MATTERS OF WHICH INVESTORS SHOULD BE AWARE.

First, some definitions. Canadian mutual funds, even if they are invested in the United States or other countries, are still considered to be Canadian property. What we are talking about here are American stocks purchased on U.S. stock exchanges (whether through a U.S. or a Canadian stock broker), and other products listed on U.S. exchanges such as WEBS and SPDRs. This will also apply to U.S. real estate, perhaps held as a vacation property, or U.S. mutual funds.

Canadian residents are taxed on their worldwide income, even if that same income may have been taxed by another country. Specifically, Canadians who invest south of the border are subject to both U.S. and Canadian income tax on their investment income from U.S. sources, which includes interest and dividend income. However, the Canada–U.S. Tax Treaty provides a measure of relief in certain cases.

Investment income is subject to a withholding rate of 30 per cent in the United States, which under the Treaty is reduced to 15 per cent for dividends and 10 per cent for interest. Exempt from these rules is interest from bank accounts and interest from government bonds and from some corporations. The gross amount of the investment income must be included in your income, even though withholding tax has been applied.

Here is the big kicker. As an investor and a taxpayer you can claim a tax credit for withholding taxes paid in another country. Thus, these U.S. taxes may then be deducted, subject to certain complex calculation limits, against the Canadian taxes that you otherwise owe on these same investments. Any tax that is not creditable against Canadian tax may be claimed as a deduction from income.

The situation with U.S. real estate gets complex really quickly, as gains on the disposition of real estate in the United States are reportable on a U.S. tax return (unlike the case for U.S. securities, which are not subject to U.S. taxes). If you own any real estate in the United States, think carefully about the headaches you will face upon disposition, and get help throughout the time that you receive rental income in the United States.

There is another hit that Canadians holding U.S. real estate face that is not generally applicable to holders of securities: U.S. estate tax. While Canada has long done away with such taxes and duties upon death, such taxes are due on property that is situated within the United States. However, a recent change to the Tax Treaty effectively only taxes gains on real estate for people whose total gross estates exceeds $1.2 million U.S.

One last factor. Unfortunately dividends that you receive from U.S. sources do not qualify for the dividend tax credit, and are thus counted similar to investment interest. Therefore, investors who require tax advantageous dividend income should focus on Canadian companies.

The Secret of Sector Funds

Tip 94

WITHIN THE WORLD OF FINANCE IT IS SAID THAT CHANGE IS THE ONLY CONSTANT. UNFORTUNATELY, THERE IS ONE EXCEPTION TO THAT RULE: THE ONLY THING THAT DOESN'T CHANGE IS THAT YOU HAVE TO PAY TAXES ON YOUR PROFITS. THUS, EVERY TIME YOU REBALANCE YOUR PORTFOLIO OR SELL A PORTION OF YOUR PORTFOLIO TO INVEST IN OTHER ATTRACTIVE INVESTMENTS, YOU HAVE TO TAKE A TAX BITE.

However, there is a solution—one refined by C.I. Mutual Funds, one of Canada's largest and fastest-growing mutual fund companies. C.I. Mutual Funds offers a product called C.I Sector Fund Limited, which is structured as a corporation, not as a mutual fund trust. This seemingly small difference allows investors to switch among the various C.I. Sector funds that are included in the C.I Sector Fund Limited, all without triggering capital gains taxes. C.I. Mutual Funds is one of several fund families that offer this feature. Remember, you still have to pay taxes, but only once you have redeemed all of your investments.

Structuring the C.I Sector Fund Limited as a corporation allows the C.I. Sector Fund to issue a number of distinct classes of shares, called sector shares. Thus, when investors switch from one single C.I. Sector fund to another fund, the transaction is not considered as a sale. By comparison, if you sold and bought a traditional mutual fund you would normally have triggered a capital gain for tax purposes.

This flexibility is well suited for investors who want to rebalance the portfolio on a regular basis, or switch among various attractive investments without triggering any capital gains. All of this can result in the saving of significant dollars in taxes.

- Investors who actively switch among various mutual funds and invest outside their RRSP should consider this product. Investments within an RRSP are already tax deferred, so there is little benefit here.

- You don't have to worry about taxes every time you sell one mutual fund and invest into another mutual fund, which means less paperwork

- C.I. Mutual Funds has a "all-star line-up" of sector funds and you won't have to pay more to invest in these funds.

- The potential for higher rates of return exists through switching among top-performing funds.

- Your book value remains constant; you always know what your cost base is for easy comparisons.

- There are higher compounded average rate of return as you get to reinvest the money you would normally have had to pay in tax.

Investors should note that occasionally the C.I Sector Fund Limited will distribute a dividend. When this occurs, investors will have to pay tax on this dividend. Also note that your investment return will be a direct result of the performance of the underlying sector shares—switching imprudently will reduce your investment returns. In short, taxable investors who trade mutual funds opportunistically should consider this, as deferring taxes can significantly increase your net worth over the long-term.

When You Disagree with Revenue Canada

Tip 95

MANY TAXPAYERS LOOK UPON ANY COMMUNICATION FROM THE CANADA CUSTOMS AND REVENUE AGENCY AS EQUIVALENT TO A LETTER FROM THE TEACHER, WHICH MUST BE OBEYED QUICKLY AND FAITHFULLY. THE REALITY SHOULD BE A LITTLE DIFFERENT. KNOWING WHERE YOU STAND CAN BOTH SAVE YOU MONEY AND CAN FURTHER EDUCATE YOU ABOUT TAXES AND THE TAX SYSTEM. IN TURN, YOU CAN USE THIS KNOWLEDGE TO REDUCE YOUR TAXES TODAY AND IN THE FUTURE.

Guiding the CCRA's actions are the "Fairness Provisions," which can be found at www.ccra-adrc.gc.ca/agency/fairness. Basically, these provisions allow the use of discretion on the part of the CCRA to cancel, reduce, or waive penalties and interest charges that they would otherwise have had to charge. These Fairness Provisions are used in extraordinary circumstances, and similarly to allow late elections. Taxpayers can make requests in writing to a district office or taxation centre. If they are still dissatisfied with the response they receive they may apply to the director of that district office or centre to review the matter.

The primary communication that you receive from the Canada Customs and Revenue Agency is the two-page Assessment Notice sent after you file your tax return. You may also be sent a Notice of Reassessment after your tax return has been filed. Check to see that everything has been entered correctly at this stage, as clerical or arithmetical errors have been known to crop up—on either your part, or by the CCRA. Remember that the CCRA is making an assessment based on the information you provided to them, which may or may not be complete.

If it is a simple error on the part of the CCRA, try the most straightforward approach—make a phone call to the number listed on your Notice. This is the best solution for the simple mistakes: a form was missed or lost, an information slip went AWOL, or an arithmetic mistake was made.

For larger matters, such as matters of interpretation, you must file a Notice of Objection, which is a letter written to the Chief of Appeals of your local district taxation office. The notice is given to the appeals branch of the local district, which reviews the situation. As a guide to the way you should structure your letter, you may want to refer to Form T400A. This is available at the above web site and, while not necessary, will give you an idea of the type of information to include. Note also that you have a specific timeframe to do all of this—either 90 days from the filing of the Notice, or one year from the date the tax return was due, whichever is later.

Remember that neither you nor the Canada Customs and Revenue Agency are right all the time. Just as they review your tax return, you should review their interpretations as well.

Ten

Maximizing Your Investment Dollar

The focus that some potential investors have on pursuing large, and often elusive returns, causes them to overlook many of the little things that go into maximizing their overall investment returns. This can range from examining the fees and returns associated with their cash holdings, to ways of purchasing their selected stocks at a discount.

Overall, one of the best resources available to investors is the Internet, which has truly levelled the playing field between small and large investors. Some of these benefits come from the sheer amount of data now available to any online investor—from stock and mutual fund quotes to investment research, most of which comes at no cost. Most of this information was unavailable on a timely basis to the individual as little as half a decade ago.

However an often-overlooked benefit of the Internet is the ability to comparison shop, incurring no long-distance phone charges, and often cutting time spent to a fraction of what was formerly necessary. In previous chapters we noted the ability to shop for mortgages online, and the ability to calculate the costs and benefits of the bells and whistles of the various products available. The same services are available when it comes to the more mundane, but still important matter of finding the bank service package that is right for you. The tools that are available to you allow you to obtain the information via computer, but more importantly to make the comparisons between the service packages.

The Internet has also given rise to a whole new range of financial institutions that exist only in cyberspace. This is another progression that began with the bill payment and investment options, and which have been offered by traditional banks for the past few years. These newer institutions offer a more limited number of banking services, and do away with the countrywide system of branch banking. In return they offer an innovative group of banking, savings, and sometimes mortgage and credit card services at interest rates that are more competitive than traditional banks, trust companies, and credit unions.

Some of the other ways to make your investment dollar go farther are far less high tech. A primary question for some investors is how to find the initial money to make an investment. This chapter outlines some of the ways to track down lost and forgotten bank accounts and other sources of funds, either using the Internet or by picking up the phone. The flip side of investing, which is accessing your credit, is covered in two ways: how to access and review your credit file to insure that your ratings are both accurate and up to date, and the best ways to maximize the use of your humble credit card.

Finding Lost Money

Tip 96

WHAT COULD BE BETTER THAN FINDING OUT THAT YOU HAVE MONEY COMING TO YOU THAT YOU HAD FORGOTTEN ABOUT, OR DIDN'T KNOW THAT YOU HAD IN THE FIRST PLACE? THIS ISN'T AS FARFETCHED AS IT SEEMS. RIGHT NOW THERE ARE APPROXIMATELY 770 000 UNCLAIMED BANK BALANCES IN CANADA (1 OUT OF 30 PEOPLE), WHICH INCLUDES MOSTLY DEPOSIT ACCOUNTS, BUT ALSO INCLUDES DRAFTS, CERTIFIED CHEQUES, DEPOSIT RECEIPTS, MONEY ORDERS, OR TRAVELLERS CHEQUES. THE TOTAL VALUE IS OVER $130 MILLION ($168 PER LOST ACCOUNT).

All of this money is held by the Bank of Canada, which acts as a custodian on behalf of the owner of the account, where there has been no activity for 10 years. Canadian banks are required to send a written notification after two years and then five years of inactivity. This applies to Canadian dollar deposits in Canadian banks, and does not include trust companies. The Bank of Canada keeps custody of all balances of over $500 indefinitely until they are claimed.

The Internet makes searching this database of "found money" very easy. Click on http://ucbswww.bank-banque-canada.ca and enter in your name, or the name of a spouse or relative where you suspect there may be some money. The same information for balances greater than $100 is published in the *Canada Gazette*, which can be found in public libraries. The Bank of Canada can also be contacted directly at:

Bank of Canada
Unclaimed Balances Services
234 Wellington Street
Ottawa, Ontario
K1A 0G9

Fax (613) 782-7802

Include the full name of the person to be searched, addresses of any past residences, and the year of death if the individual is deceased.

If you are fortunate enough to discover any missing money, claiming it is relatively straightforward. You will need to prove both your identity and the connection with the account. This can include an original bank passbook or statement, or proof that you resided at the address noted in the account. If you are an heir you will need documentation of that status. Complete the one-page claim form, found on the Internet site. You also need to include your signature and authorization from the financial institution where the account originally was held. Once you have submitted the form to the Bank of Canada, the claim is typically paid in a month or two. There are no fees to either search the database or to claim the balance. However there might be fees that owners will have to pay to have their signatures notarized or authenticated.

If you want to do a broader search including U.S. balances, one source is www.foundmoney.com. While initial searches on this site are free, complete details must be paid for.

Know Your Credit File

Tip 97

DO YOU CROSS YOUR FINGERS EVERY TIME YOU ASK YOUR BANKER TO BORROW MONEY OR APPLY FOR CREDIT? WOULDN'T YOU BE MORE COMFORTABLE IF YOU KNEW HOW GOOD YOUR CREDIT WAS BEFORE YOU WENT IN? IT'S WISE TO FIND OUT YOUR CREDIT RATING, BOTH FOR YOUR OWN PERSONAL KNOWLEDGE, AND ALSO TO MAKE SURE THAT IT IS CORRECT. THIS IS IMPORTANT BECAUSE YOUR CREDIT RATING IS A MAJOR INFLUENCE ON YOUR ABILITY TO APPLY FOR CREDIT AT FAVOURABLE TERMS, EITHER FOR CREDIT CARDS, LOANS FOR INVESTMENT, OR OBTAINING A MORTGAGE.

In Canada, there are two main credit agencies that records your borrowing history. They are Equifax Canada Inc., and Trans Union of Canada Inc. It is important that you check these files every few years. It is a simple process, and these agencies are required by law to show you your credit history upon request, and at no charge. The contacts are:

Equifax Canada Inc.
Consumer Relations Department
Box 190
Jean Talon Station
Montreal, Quebec
H1S 2Z2

Phone: 1-800-465-7166 or (514) 493-2314

Trans Union of Canada Inc.
Consumers Relation Centre
Box 338 LCD 1
Hamilton, Ontario
L8L 7W2

Phone: 1-800-663-9980 or (905) 525-4420

In each case include your name, address, date of birth, phone number, and a photocopy of two pieces of identification with your signature on it. Your report should arrive in a few weeks. Because of security concerns, reports are not given out over the phone or the Internet.

A report will be assigned a numerical rating, from one to nine, based on the speed that past payments have been made. If you receive a rating of one it means payments have been made either on time or within 30 days of the due date, which is good. If you receive a rating of nine it means the debt has been placed with a collection agency. Aside from giving you an interesting picture of your personal finances, your credit report will mention information in the public record on bankruptcies and judgements, actions by third party collection agencies, and past and current credit history. This is the part that is frequently incorrect, thus you want to make sure that all the information applies to you.

If mistakes were made in your credit files you can supply any documentation necessary to clarify inaccuracies. As well, notes can be appended to your file to explain past delinquencies or other problems. All of this is time well spent to avoid future surprises.

Getting Extra Mileage
from Your Credit Card

Tip 98

CREDIT CARDS ARE JUST A LITTLE BIT OF PLASTIC, BUT THEY MAKE A BIG DIFFER-ENCE IN PEOPLE'S LIVES. WHEN IT COMES TO CREDIT CARDS, EVERYBODY SEEMS TO HAVE DIFFERENT NEEDS, WHICH IS WHY BANKS AND CREDIT UNIONS OFFER A WIDE SELECTION OF CARDS TO SUIT YOUR LIFESTYLE.

The advantages of credit cards include worldwide use, ABM banking access, and an interest-free period for new purchases if you repay the balance by the due date. They can also offer high credit limits, itemized monthly statements, and a fraud-monitoring feature. The more elaborate cards also offer various insurance products and other features, although these cards may charge an annual fee. Most financial companies provide a simple card with no fee, and other cards with additional options and fees.

The following is a list of some the more popular VISA and MasterCard cards that people use. Financial institutions are always coming up with new types of credit cards. To receive a complete list check with your financial institution (the Royal Bank's site at www.royalbank.com, for example, has a "cardselector" for choosing between the bank's normal, premium, and affinity credit cards) or check the links at www.moneycanada.com.

- CIBC's Dividend Platinum VISA works like a good dividend-paying stock. You can earn up to 2 per cent in cash dividends when you use this card. Each December you will receive your dividend dollars that you can use to build your investments or pay off the balance of your card.

- CIBC's Aerogold VISA allows you to collect points for you next trip. When you use this credit card you are automatically enrolled in Aeroplan—Air Canada's frequent flyer program. Every dollar you spend on this credit card will earn you Aeroplan miles that you can use to fly Air Canada or any partner in the Star Alliance group.

- TD's GM VISA credit card allows you to receive 5 per cent of your purchases in GM Card earnings. These earnings can be applied towards the purchase or lease of any eligible GM car, truck, or van. There is no annual fee for this card, and there are limits—you can only accumulate up to $500 a year for the purchase of a vehicle. Citibank offers a similar card you can use for any vehicle.

- First time homebuyers can find it difficult to save for their first home. With the Bank of Montreal FirstHome Program you can accumulate dollars every time you use your MasterCard credit card.

Consumers should have a credit card to build a credit history, which can be a valuable asset when you eventually apply for a loan. Using credit prudently will allow you to manage you monthly expenditures efficiently and effectively while earning points or credit for a new car, your retirement, or a vacation. Check with your financial institution and make sure that you have the best credit card for your needs.

Reducing Your Bank Fees

Tip 99

IF YOU WANT TO START A CONVERSATION AT A PARTY, YOU HAVE TWO OPEN-
ING GAMBITS. YOU CAN ASK FOR STOCK MARKET ADVICE, OR YOU CAN
COMPLAIN ABOUT BANK SERVICE FEES. EITHER WAY, YOU ARE LIABLE TO GET
SOME PRETTY STRONG OPINIONS.

While we might still have memories of banks giving free calendars, and tellers who had
endless time to chat and help us for free, all we now hear is the beep of the ATM, and we
pay service fees for the privilege. Thus the issue is how to pick the best plan, which is no
easy task considering that the Bank of Montreal, for example, has a dozen different service plans.

One of the best sources for comparison information comes from Industry Canada. Their
Office of Consumer Affairs has produced a detailed financial service charges calculator that
lets you understand how you can use your bank to your own advantage. More importantly,
it lets you make comparisons among 16 different financial institutions, including the major
banks as well as such institutions as Citizens Bank, HSBC, Metro Credit Union, and
VanCity. Gather your most recent bank statements and go to the web site at
www.strategis.ic.gc.ca/SSG/ca00669e.html. Enter your monthly transaction habits (lowest
balance, the number of cheques that you write), the number and locations of the
withdrawals that you make, how you pay your bills using your financial institution, the
number of transfers you make between accounts, and any other financial transactions you
may undertake. Punch in the financial institution you now use, or any other that you are

thinking of using, and out comes a summary of your total fees, including INTERAC fees, in each of the institution's service plans.

Once you make the appropriate choice of plans, you can still cut back on fees by trying the following:

- If you are performing a transaction at a branch (such as bill payment), or if your financial service needs are minimal, consider using that institution's ATM, which usually has a lower fee.

- Try to limit the use of another financial institution's ATM machines, which usually have an extra fee involved.

- While some institutions offer no-fee packages if a minimum balance is maintained in your account, compare the savings of service fees to the higher interest that is foregone if a better savings vehicle is chosen.

- Most institutions offer attractive senior packages, with the definition of senior often applying at age 59 or 60. At the other end of the spectrum, youth plans are available offering minimal or no fees.

- Look at the costs associated with phone banking or Internet banking, if available at your institution. These banking options can be a major time saver, even if fee differences are minimal.

Remember a dollar saved is like two dollars earned before tax.

Going Direct with Internet Banking

Tip 100

EVENTUALLY THE CORNER BANK MAY BE REPLACED WITH AN AUTOMATIC TELLER MACHINE (ATM), BUT THIS IS FAR FROM THE LAST CHANGE THAT WILL BE SEEN TO TRADITIONAL BANKS. THE LATEST TREND IN THE FINANCIAL SERVICES INDUSTRY IS FINANCIAL INSTITUTIONS THAT EXIST ONLY IN CYBERSPACE, WITHOUT A "BRICKS AND MORTAR" LOCATION. THESE BANKS CAN OFFER THEIR CUSTOMERS MANY ADVANTAGES, EVEN IF THEY DO LACK THE PERSONAL TOUCH.

These virtual banks differ from one another, and specifics about their services change all the time. However, there are some common elements. Interest rates are typically very high, and service fees are non-existent. Accounts are also insured for the traditional $60 000 by the Canada Deposit Insurance Corporation (CDIC). In many cases, the cyberbank is backed by a larger bricks and mortar financial institution (for example, President's Choice Financial is supported by the Canadian Imperial Bank of Commerce). On the downside, the types of accounts available at any Internet bank are very limited. While most of the big five banks offer three or more different chequing accounts, and a similar number of savings accounts, Internet banks usually offer one basic savings account and one basic chequing account. More generally, the full range of services offered by financial institutions, including money orders, ATM services, and foreign currency accounts, are not always available.

Here are the major players:

- President's Choice Financial is one of the most visible of the new Internet Banks. They offer a wide selection of services, including bill payment, Visa cards, and mortgages. A differentiating feature of all of these services is a tie-in with their PC point's plan, which is redeemable for free groceries at Loblaws stores. They are also the least "virtual" of these new banks, as some Loblaws stores have small PC Financial stores within them, with ATMs and staff to answer questions. Contact www.preschoicefinancial.com, or 1-888-872-4724.

- ING Direct is also a highly visible virtual bank, offering a range of its own ATMs in addition to phone and Internet banking. The backing financial institution is ING Bank of Canada, and the web contact is www.ingdirect.ca, or 1-800-ING-DIRECT.

- Finactive offers a daily interest savings account, with the financial backing of Imperial Life Assurance Company. Contact www.finactive.com or 1-888-777-0700.

- Manulife Bank offers a range of accounts. Contact www.manulifebank.com or 1-877-765-2265.

- M.R.S. Trust Company offers account services via financial advisors. The backing institution is M.R.S. Trust Company, which is a subsidiary of Mackenzie Financial Corp. Contact www.mrs.com or 1-800-387-2087.

While these institutions offer much, it is important to keep in mind that they are not a substitute for investing in instruments that pay higher interest rates, or offer the potential for a greater return. They are, instead, a place to hold your short-term cash to pay your short-term obligations. You don't want to become so enamoured of these new banks that you lose sight of their role in your financial plan.

Dividend Reinvestment Plans
Make You Money!

Tip 101

BUYING STOCKS WITHOUT A BROKERAGE COMMISSION: WHAT COULD BE BETTER THAN THAT? CALLED DIVIDEND REINVESTMENT PLANS (DRIPS), THESE PLANS ALLOW INVESTORS TO BUY STOCK AND REINVEST DIVIDEND PAYMENTS IN MORE STOCK, DIRECTLY THROUGH THE ISSUING COMPANY. THIS BYPASSES A TRADITIONAL STOCKBROKER, AND SAVES ON THE COMMISSIONS THAT WOULD OTHERWISE BE CHARGED TO BUY OR TO SELL. THE COMPANIES THAT PARTICI-PATE IN THESE PLANS ARE TYPICALLY WELL ESTABLISHED, BLUE CHIP FIRMS THAT PAY DIVIDENDS, AND INCLUDE CANADIAN BANKS SUCH AS THE ROYAL BANK OF CANADA AND THE CANADIAN IMPERIAL BANK OF COMMERCE, RESOURCE FIRMS SUCH AS SUNCOR AND PETRO CANADA, UTILITIES SUCH AS BELL CANADA, AND MANUFACTURERS SUCH AS DOFASCO.

There are other potential benefits to the investor of participating in these programs. The start-up costs are minimal, as you can buy as little as one share in a company. This means that you can put together a reasonably diversified portfolio of stocks for under $1000. Reinvesting dividends is also a wonderful forced savings plan, providing more discipline to your investing approach, and forcing a long-term perspective to your investment strategy. While stocks in this program can be sold, also on a commission-free basis, there is more paperwork involved than making a traditional sell decision with a broker. Thus, dividend reinvestment plans are not for short-term investor looking to flip an investment quickly.

The time and paperwork involved in these plans is the biggest drawback. Initial shares must be registered in your name, not the name of a brokerage firm. Enrolment in these plans involves filling in application forms from the company's trustee. You should figure on making a few phone calls, completing some forms, and waiting a month or so.

Finding out about these deals is easy. While companies sign on and drop out of these programs all the time, there are numerous up-to-date listings that appear in weekend newspapers and magazines (*The Canadian Money Saver* magazine keeps up with this field, and can be accessed at www.canadianmoneysaver.ca). But this is a backward approach that focusses more on the discount available and less on the company in which you are investing. You are better off doing the research on the company first, to ensure that the stock is a sound investment for you. Then, check the last page of the company's annual report to find out if such a program is offered. If you are in doubt, call the firm's shareholder relations department, which is also listed in the annual report, and which keeps current on all of the details of the plan. Once you have signed up there is no further paperwork required. If you invest in a sound company with long-term growth potential, a DRIP is an option you should consider.

Glossary

Absorbed: An issue is absorbed when it has been entirely sold to the public.

Account Statement: A record that summarizes all transactions in an investor's account. Statements have to be provided to investors at least quarterly. However, some firms provide statements on a monthly basis.

Accrued Interest: Interest accumulated on a bond since the last interest payment.

Acquisition: When one corporation acquires a controlling interest in another corporation.

Across the Board: A movement – either up or down – in the stock market that affects almost all the stocks. For example, if almost all the stocks on a stock exchange appreciated in value than you would say "the movement was across the board."

Active Market: When a stock or a stock market experiences heavy trading volume.

ADR (American Depository Receipt): A receipt for shares of a foreign-based company. These receipts are traded on an American stock exchange.

Affiliated Company: A company that has less than 50 per cent of its shares owned by another company (See Subsidiary.)

After-Tax Real Rate of Return: The rate of return earned by aninvestor after deducting the tax expense and the rate of inflation. This number should be positive if you are making good investments.

All Time Periods (ATP) Chart: A combination of tables that illustrates the historical performance of a mutual fund.

Alternative Minimum Tax (AMT): A tax aimed at preventing affluent investors from using tax shelters to avoid paying income tax.

Analyst: An individual who researches corporations, industry groups, and the stock market to make buy and sell recommendations for investors.

Annual Meeting: A stockholder meeting that is held yearly. This meeting is held to allow corporate executives to report on the year's results, to elect the board of directors, and to transact any other business outstanding.

Annual Report: The formal financial statements issued by the company to shareholders after the company's year end.

Annuity: A contract between a life insurance company and an investor which guarantees income for a predefined period.

Arrears: Dividends that weren't paid when due but are still owed to shareholders. This is a common feature of preferred shares.

Asset Allocation: The division of investment funds among various types of investment categories.

Assets: All the valuables of a corporation or individual.

Average Cost: The average cost of acquiring an investment. For example, if an investor bought 100 shares at $50 each and 100 shares at $100 each, the average cost would be 100 × $50 plus 100 × $100 divided by 200, which is equal to $75 per share. The taxable capital gain for an investment is the selling price minus the average cost.

Averaging Down: Investing in additional securities of a particular investment to reduce your average cost.

Back Office: Those divisions at a broker-dealer that are not directly involved in sales or trading. These back office departments include accounting and record keeping.

Back-End Load: A fee that an investor pays when withdrawing money from an investment; this is also called a "deferred sales charge."

Balance Sheet: A financial statement disclosing a corporation's assets, liabilities, and owners' equity as of a particular date.

Bankrupt: The legal status of a corporation (or an individual) that hasn't been able to pay its debts in an orderly fashion.

Basis Point: A financial industry term: 1/100th of 1 per cent is 1 basis point.

Bear: An investor who expects the market will decline.

Bear Market: A declining capital market.

Bell: A signal that indicates that trading on a major stock exchange has either opened or closed.

Bellwether Security: A stock that is perceived as an indicator of the overall stock market's direction. Bell Canada, for example, is considered a bellwether stock in Canada.

Beneficiary: A person who is, or will be, the recipient of the proceeds of money held by an individual in the event of death.

Bid and Ask: A bid is the highest price a buyer is willing to pay for a security. An ask is the lowest price a seller is willing to accept for the security.

Big Board: Industry lingo for the New York Stock Exchange.

Black Monday: Monday, October 19, 1987. This was the day when the Dow Jones Industrial Average fell a record 508 points.

Block Trade: A large amount of a stock sold or bought as a single unit.

Blue Chip: A "brand name" leading company with an established record of earnings and dividend payments. The term blue chip is generated from the card game of poker, in which the blue chips are the most valuable. Blue-chip companies are the largest and most valuable companies.

Board Lot: A regular trading unit (number of shares) that has been uniformly established by stock exchanges.

Bond: A certificate proving a debt on which the issuer has a legal obligation to pay the debt holder an interest payment and repay the loan at maturity.

Book Value: The value of the assets belonging to the shareholders of a company after the creditors have been paid.

Bottom-Up Approach to Investing: An investment method where an investor will look for individual stocks that exhibit value. This approach assumes that an individual company's stock can do well, even though its industry group may not.

Broker: An individual who acts as an agent to facilitate the trade of securities for buyers and sellers. Brokers charge a fee for their services.

Bull: An investor who expects an increase in capital markets.

Bull Market: An increasing capital market.

Buy Order: An order placed with your broker to purchase a specified number of shares in a company at a particular price.

Buying on Margin: Buying securities on credit after established a margin account at a brokerage firm.

Call: An option that gives the holder the right, but not the obligation, to buy a specific number of shares or another commodity at a specified price within a specified time period.

Canadian Investor Protection Fund: A protection fund established by the stock exchanges and the Investment Dealers Association (IDA) to protect investors from losses resulting from the failure of a member firm.

Capital Gain or Loss: The profit or loss generated from the sale of an investment.

Capital Stock: All shares that represent ownership of a corporation, including preferred and common stock.

Closed-end Mutual Fund: A mutual fund with a limited number of shares issued. When these shares have been sold, the fund is closed.

Commission: The fee charged by an individual who sells investments for buying or selling these investments.

Common Stock: A security that represents ownership in a company.

Compounded Rates of Return: Interest and capital gains accumulated over a period of time, which are added to the original investment as a percentage of the original investment.

Conglomerate: A corporation that operates in a variety of different industries.

Consumer Price Index (CPI): A measure of price changes in consumer goods.

Correction: An upward movement in the price of an individual stock or the stock market after a downward movement.

Coupon: A certificate entitling the owner to an interest payment from the bond issuer.

Crash: A steep drop in stock prices.

Credit Rating: An assessment of an individual's credit history and their future ability to pay their debt obligations.

Current Yield: The annual income (interest and dividends) received from a security throughout the year, divided by the current market value of the security.

Cyclical Stock: A stock that is very sensitive to changes in economic conditions.

Day Order: An order to buy or sell a stock that is valid only for the trading day the order is given.

Day Trade: To purchase and sell a stock in within the same day.

Debenture: Similar to a bond, but the collateral behind the debenture is only the general earning power of the company.

Default: A bond is considered in default when the issuer is no longer able to make regular interest payments. Bankruptcy may result from a company defaulting on its bond obligations.

Defensive Stock: The stock of a corporation with an excellent record of stable profits and dividend payments. Defensive stocks tend to outperform during bear markets.

Derivative Instrument: A financial instrument whose price is based on the value of another security.

Disposable Income: Income that is left after paying taxes, food, clothing, transportation, and shelter. The remainder can be saved or spent.

Distributions: Money received from your investments; either dividends or capital gains from stocks or income, dividends, and capital gains from mutual funds.

Diversification: Investing in more than one security or asset class in order to reduce the overall risk.

Dividend: A payment made by a corporation to shareholders from the company's profits. There is no legal obligation to pay a dividend on common shares.

Dollar Cost Averaging: Investing a fixed dollar amount into an investment on a regular basis to take advantage of volatility.

DJIA (Dow Jones Industrial Average): Average of the prices of 30 well-known, predominantly blue-chip, industrial stocks.

Earnings Momentum: A corporation's earnings per share that is continuously increasing from one period to the next.

Earnings per Share: The portion of the company's profits that can be attributed to one common share. If the company earned $1000 and had 1000 shares outstanding, the earnings per share would be $1.

Economic Indicators: Key statistics indicating the direction of the overall economy.

Equity: An ownership interest in a business or corporation.

Expense Ratio: The total fees paid by mutual fund investors, stated as a percentage of the total investment.

Fiscal Year or Period: A corporation's accounting year. A corporation's tax year can end in any month; an individual's tax year ends on December 31.

Fixed Annuity: An annuity that works the same way a variable annuity does except its value and paid-out amount are fixed. Typically these policies offer a stock fund, a bond fund, and a money market fund.

Fixed Income Securities: Investments that generate a predictable and consistent flow of income or returns for investors. Fixed income investments include money market mutual funds, Canadian bond funds, and international bond funds.

Forecasting: Predicting future stock market trends using existing data.

Front Office: A term used to identify personnel who deal directly with the public for a brokerage firm.

Front-End Load: A sales charge charged at the time of purchase of an investment.

Fundamental Analysis: The evaluation of a common stock based on the attractiveness of the company's financial statements.

Futures Contract: An agreement to either take or make delivery of a standardized commodity on a particular date.

Glamour Stock: Stocks that achieve a wide following because they consistently produce higher sales and earnings over a long-term.

GNP (Gross National Product): The total value of goods and services produced by the economy in a given period. GNP is closely related to Gross Domestic Product (GDP).

Going Public (IPO): An industry term used to describe the initial public offering (IPO) or sale of shares of a privately held corporation to the public.

Graham and Dodd Method of Investing: This is an investment theory established in the 1930s by Benjamin Graham and David Dodd that is summarized in their book *Security Analysis*. Graham and Dodd believed that investors should buy stocks in companies that have undervalued assets.

Guaranteed Investment Certificate (GIC): A deposit investment available at all major banks and trust companies. GICs are non-redeemable until maturity and offer a predetermined rate of interest.

Hedge Fund: A specialized open investment company that has the ability to use leverage, options, short selling or other investment techniques.

High Flyer: A very speculative and high risk stock that moves up or down considerably in the short-term.

High Grade Bond: A bond that is rated "AAA" or "AA" by Moody's or Standard & Poor's rating services.

High Yield Bond: A bond that is rated "BB" or lower by Moody's or Standard & Poor's rating services. These bonds pay a higher yield to offset the greater risk.

Home Run: A large gain obtained by an investor in a short time period.

Income statement: A financial statement that discloses the corporation's sales revenue, expenditures, and profits during the fiscal period.

Index: A measure that indicates the status of a group of companies or investments. For example, the TSE 300 measures the performance of 300 of Canada's largest publicly traded companies.

Index Fund: A mutual fund that buys securities to match the securities that comprise a broad-based index such as the S&P 500 index.

Inflation: The rise in the prices of goods and services.

Interest: Fee (or rent) charged by a lender to a borrower for the use of the lender's money.

Investment: The use of money to generate more money, to receive income, dividends, or capital gains.

Investment Counsellor: An individual who is qualified to give investment advice for a fee.

Leverage: The strategy of borrowing money to invest. Investors hope to earn more on the invested money than they had to pay to borrow it.

Liabilities: The debts of a company.

Limit Order: An order to buy or sell a security at a particular price or better. If a limit order can't be executed at that price or better, the order won't be executed. A specific time limit may be applied to the order.

Load: The portion of the investment that is used to pay selling expenses. Loads are common in front-end load mutual funds.

Macroeconomics: Analysis of the overall economy using information such as unemployment, inflation, production, and price levels.

Majority Shareholder: A shareholder who controls more than half of the outstanding voting shares of a company.

Management Fee: An expense paid by a mutual fund to the investment advisor for managing the portfolio investments.

Negative Cash Flow: An accounting period where a company spends more cash than it receives.

Net Asset Value (NAV): The net asset value of a mutual fund is the actual value of each share. This is calculated by dividing the total value of the fund by the number of shares outstanding.

New York Stock Exchange (NYSE): The oldest and largest stock exchange in the United States. This stock exchange is commonly referred to as the "Big Board" or "The Exchange".

No Transaction Fee (NTF) Program: A program that allows investors to buy hundreds of different no-load funds within the same account without paying any transaction fees. The program is so popular that even full-service brokerage firms are beginning to follow this practice.

No-load Funds: Mutual funds that can be purchased, sold, and owned without any commission charges. The only charges involved are management fees. Shares are sold at the net asset value price, and no salesperson is paid to sell the shares.

Open-end Mutual Fund: A mutual fund that imposes no limit on the number of shares that can be issued, and thus will issue and redeem shares at an investor's request.

Overvalued: A security whose price is not justified by its future prospects and thus should eventually decline.

P/E Ratio: The price of a stock divided by the yearly earnings per share. It compares the price of a stock relative to its earnings, which is important to know when you compare one stock to another. It is also important in determining if a stock is under- or over-priced relative to other stocks.

Penny Stock: A stock that is priced at less than $1 a share. Penny stocks are very volatile and speculative.

Privately Held Company: A company whose shares are not publicly traded. Privately held stock is issued to a small number of shareholders, and the value or price of the stock is usually determined by comparisons with other similar companies, using factors such as earnings and gross income.

Pro-forma Financial Statements: Financial statements that are used to project the estimated financial results of a new company. They consist of an income statement, balance sheet, and cash flow statement.

Prospectus: A document that details all material information about a mutual fund or security being issued. A prospectus must be given to all buyers and potential buyers of the new issue.

Qualified Plans: A plan that allows an individual to make a pre-tax deposit and have income tax deferred. A registered company pension plan allows employees to deposit part of their incomes in the plan with the tax-deferred privilege. A registered retirement savings plan (RRSP) is the only other type of qualified plan. An individual can select from a large number of different investments.

Quantitative Analysis: The study and analysis of numerical financial information for the basis of decision making. The principle of quantitative theory is that everything is expressed in measurable form and is therefore also predictable. Investors who use this theory believe that by studying specific market data they can accurately predict the market's movements.

Rally: A stock market rise that follows a period of stock market decline .

Relative Strength: A graphic illustration of the percentage (or fractional) difference between the price of a security and an index (or any other security). If the security and index rise and fall equally at the same time, the graph would be a straight line.

RESP (Registered Education Savings Plan): An investment vehicle for saving for your child's post-secondary education. Contributions made to RESPs aren't deductible for tax purposes, but the income earned in the plan grows tax-free.

Return on Investment (ROI): A company's ROI can be calculated by dividing the net income by the amount of capital invested in the company. There are two ways to increase ROI: reduce expenses, or increase sales. Individual ROI is equal to net proceeds of investment divided by initial investment.

Risk: A measurable possibility of losing money.

RRIF (Registered Retirement Income Fund): An income plan that can be purchased at any time and that provides a stream of income.

RRSP (Registered Retirement Savings Plan): A savings plan that allows individuals who have not reached age 69 to set aside money for retirement within certain limits.

Sales Charges: Several purchase options are available when you buy mutual funds: Back-end load (also referred to as deferred sales charge or redemption charge) means a charge may be applied when you sell mutual fund units, payable to the mutual fund company. Front-end load means the sales charge is applied at the time you purchase mutual fund units, payable to the mutual fund company. A no-load fund doesn't charge a sales fee for buying and selling your shares.

Secondary Market: Any market where previously issued securities are traded. The Toronto Stock Exchange (TSE) is the best-known example in Canada. Here investors can buy and sell stocks from each other through the Exchange.

Shareholders' Equity: The ownership interest in the firm by common shareholders. The shareholders' or owners' equity in the firm is equal to the firm's assets minus the firm's liabilities.

Speciality Fund: A mutual fund that invests in the stocks of a particular industry, such as the oil and gas, technology, or real estate industry.

Stock: See Common Stock.

Subsidiary: A company that is owned by another company through the ownership of 50 per cent or more of the common shares outstanding.

Take a Flier: Investing in a security while having the full knowledge that the investment is highly risky.

Target Savings Goal (TSG): The amount of money required each year to build a portfolio large enough to support your preferred standard of living at retirement.

Technical Analysis: Using charts to read the price history and other statistical patterns of stocks or mutual funds. Many investors and most professionals use these charts to make investment decisions. A technical analyst is also known as a chartist.

Total Return: The percentage return of a portfolio, which includes dividends, interest, and capital gains. Total return is also known as portfolio performance.

Underwriter: A brokerage firm that handles the process of offering a company's stock to the public through an initial public offering.

Value Manager: A manager who searches for undervalued stocks that are priced below what the manager actually thinks they're worth. The goal of the value-oriented manager is to sell at a profit once the market realizes the stock's true value.

Variable Annuity: An annuity that works the same way a fixed annuity does except its value and paid-out amount vary according to the performance of a portfolio of mutual funds from which the contract holder can select.

Vos Value Rating (VVR): Measures a mutual fund's performance, underlying risk, and balance between risk and reward.

Withholding: The keeping back of either earned income, or interest or dividend payment by an employer or institution for remittance to Revenue Canada.

Yield: The percentage return on an investment.

Zero-coupon Bond: A bond that provides no annual or semi-annual interest payments, and is issued at a fraction of its par value.

Index